The

Resources And Projects

Book

A Student Guide to Design and Technology

Ollie Kasicki

 DELMAR PUBLISHERS INC.

NOTICE TO THE READER

To Min, Alex, Oliver and Lewis

Delmar Staff
New Product Acquisition Specialist: Mark Huth
Project Editor: Carol Micheli
Production Coordinator: Wendy Troeger

For information, address Delmar Publishers Inc.
2 Computer Drive West, Box 15-015
Albany, New York 12212

Printed in the United States of America
published simultaneously in Canada
by Nelson Canada,
a division of The Thomson Corporation

10   9   8   7   6   5   4   3   2   1

ISBN: 0-8273-5265-4

Acknowledgments

The author and publishers are grateful to the following for permission to reproduce copyright photographs:
J. Allen Cash, p. 54 *(3 pictures)*; John Urling Clark, p. 36 *(left)*, 39 *(left)*, 73; Connolly Leather, p. 58 *(bottom right)*; Dunlop Slazenger, p. 58 *(top right)*; Greg Evans Photo Library, p. 30 *(left, top center and center)*, 53; Prodeepta Das, p. 10 *(top left)*, 55 *(2 pictures)*; Derek Henderson Photography, p. 45; Chris Ridgers Photography, p. 10 *(top right and bottom right)*, 18, 21 *(left)*, 39 *(right)*, 58 *(center right)*, 69, 72; Rover Group, p. 36 *(right)*; Science Photo Library, p. 54, 55 *(5 pictures)*, 58 *(top left)*, 58 *(bottom right)*; Scope Optics, p. 58 *(top center)*, Tony Stone Associates/Jon Riley, p. 54 *(2 pictures)*, Phil Warren, Tyne Timbers, p. 52; Zefa, p. 54 *(2 pictures)*.

Cartoons by Steve Donald, Simon Donald, Graham Dury, Simon Thorp, Rob Snow.

CONTENTS

WHAT IS TECHNOLOGY?

Technology is the use of all human knowledge. We use technology all the time. Anything which is man-made is the result of technology. The things we do, and the way we go about them are the result of technology. Our local surroundings and the world environment have been changed by technology

Technology is not new. It has been around ever since the human race began making and improving simple tools, building better places to live and inventing new ways to communicate.

Technology is a process. The human race is learning more every day. All this knowledge is added to what we already know. **Technology is growing all the time.** The human race has been on Earth for about three million years. In the last 10,000 years or so technology has really taken off.

Every so often a huge discovery is made which gives technology a real boost. This new knowledge can be used in ways which could not even have been imagined before. Here are some examples:

- ▶ discovering fire
- ▶ making stone tools
- ▶ the printing press
- ▶ the steam engine
- ▶ X-rays
- ▶ electricity
- ▶ television
- ▶ the microchip

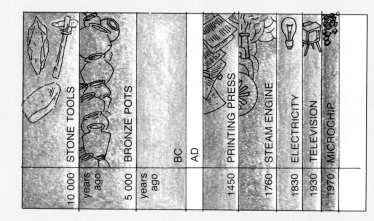

STONE TOOLS	BRONZE POTS	BC	AD	PRINTING PRESS	STEAM ENGINE	ELECTRICITY	TELEVISION	MICROCHIP
10 000 years ago	5 000 years ago			1450	1760	1830	1930	1970

Can you think of any other major discoveries? How have these discoveries changed the way we live now?

We can trace the technology in everyday objects by investigating them. Think about all the things that you would need to know before you could make an electric coffee maker, a camera or a telephone director.

Things are not made the way they are by chance. Someone decided to make them that way. **Someone who spends time and effort deciding how something should work or look is called a designer.** Their decision is called a design.

Designers learn how to make judgements so that they can make good designs. They judge their own work and the work of other people to help them with their ideas.

Designers have to know how to make things. They need to know about different materials. They need to know how things work.

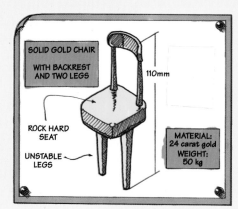

SOLID GOLD CHAIR
WITH BACKREST
AND TWO LEGS

110mm

ROCK HARD SEAT

UNSTABLE LEGS

MATERIAL: 24 carat gold
WEIGHT: 50 kg

Designers cannot do anything they like. They have to think about the cost, how long things need to last and many other things. **The rules which control what designers can do are called constraints.**

Designers often work in teams. Different experts work together using a master plan which everyone can follow. Learning to work in a team is a very important part of design and technology.

Once designers have sorted out their ideas they have to explain them to the people who will carry out the plans. This is called **communicating designs**. Designers use drawings, models, words, films and other ways to communicate their ideas.

Through design and technology you will have a better understanding of the world which we have created. You will learn to judge the way people do things. And in the future you will be able to help to make the world a better place.

MANAGING YOUR WORK

As you get older you will find that the design tasks which you are expected to do get more complicated. You will have to plan your work and organize yourself so that you can finish your work on time and produce good results.

A good work plan will help you. It will show you how much time you can spend on the different parts of the job and the materials you will need in order to finish the job.

The work plan below shows how Jimmy organizes his morning so that he can do all his jobs and still get to school on time.

START	TIME	TASKS	RESOURCES
7.00			
	5 mins	GET UP AND GET DRESSED	ALARM CLOCK CLOTHES
7.05			
	5 mins	GO TO NEWSAGENT	BIKE NEWSPAPER SACK
7.10			
	10 mins	COLLECT AND SORT PAPERS	PAPERS ADDRESSES
7.20			
	60 mins	DELIVER PAPERS	PAPERS/BIKE MAP
8.20			
	5 mins	RETURN HOME	BIKE
8.25			
	15 mins	EAT BREAKFAST	FOOD
8.40			
	15 mins	WALK TO SCHOOL	SCHOOL BAG
8.55			
	5 mins	WAIT FOR BELL	SCHOOL YARD
9.00	DEADLINE		

Priorities

Some resources are more important than others. There may not be enough money or time to do everything you would like. **A list of priorities** will help you to decide what you could manage without and what you definitely must have. The most important things go at the top of your priority list.

Estimates

Very often it is impossible to know how long a job will take, especially if it is something you haven't done before. In this case you must make a guess. A useful guess is based on advice or by comparing a job to a similar task. This is called making an **estimate**.

The best laid plans go wrong

What happens when Jimmy's bike gets a flat or he oversleeps his alarm?
At any time he can make adjustments to his **timeplan** and decide where his priorities are. Will he miss breakfast? Could he get the bus to school? It is always a good idea to keep a little time in reserve when you do your work plan in case of emergencies.

LOOKING FOR NEEDS AND OPPORTUNITIES

Don't think of it as a problem.
Think of it as an opportunity.

Needs and opportunities are all around. How many things do you have because you need to have them? How many things have you done because you had the opportunity to do them?

We fill our lives with lots of junk. Stuff we don't really need, things which are not really worth doing. Good designers investigate the possibilities before going ahead with an idea. **Investigating and making judgements** is called **evaluating**.

Is it really wanted?

Not everyone feels the same way about things. Find out people's views by using opinion polls or surveys.

Caring for the environment

In the past, designers thought mainly about people. Today they must think about the needs of the planet Earth. New designs have to use less energy, fewer resources, make less mess and be less harmful to the planet.

Needs and opportunities must:

▶ be wanted

▶ be environmentally friendly

▶ be socially acceptable

▶ not create new problems.

Good for one and all?

People can be very selfish and not think about others. Designers must think about the needs of the population as well as the needs of individual people.

New problems for old

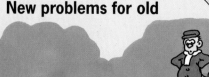

Solving one problem can create another. New things which are created have to fit in with everything which has been made before. Good designers think about the likely effects of their designs.

Designers are always asking questions about things when they are **evaluating**.

Designers look at their own work as well as the work of other people. They evaluate ideas from other countries. They examine things which were made in the past. They look at the way people do things as well as the things that they make. They look at the way things have changed our lives.

Designers evaluate to find needs and opportunities. They also evaluate to get new ideas and to improve their own work.

Opinion polls and fair tests may help you to evaluate design ideas.

I HAVE LOOKED AT THE FACTS, AND YOUR BURGERS HAVE TERRIBLE INGREDIENTS, LOOK HORRIBLE AND ARE EXPENSIVE. IN FUTURE I SUGGEST YOU MAKE THEM LIKE THIS: HEALTHY INGREDIENTS, GOOD-LOOKING AND CHEAPER!

Opinion polls

DO YOU THINK WE NEED AN ADVENTURE PLAYGROUND?

It is worth asking friends, teachers and relatives what they think about your work. If you get a lot of different answers then it might be worth doing an opinion poll. Ask a group of people the same questions and see how they answer.

Fair tests

Sometimes it may be difficult to decide which is the best way of doing something. You can compare the two things by doing a fair test.

EQUAL WEIGHTS

DIFFERENT BAGS

You can be judge

Look at your work in three ways. These are some of the questions you could ask yourself:

1 How did I go about my work?

Did I work safely and carefully?

Did I allow enough time?

Did I plan properly?

Did I need help?

Did I learn anything new?

2 What do I think about the thing I have made?

How well is it made?

Did I use the best materials?

Does it work?

Does it look good?

Could I make any improvements?

3 What are the likely effects of my work?

Does it do the job it is supposed to?

Is it going to last?

Would anyone else want it?

Is it environmentally friendly?

Will it cause problems?

BUSINESS OPPORTUNITIES

People go into business to make money. A successful business will make enough to pay the workforce, pay all the bills and still have some money left over. This extra money is called the **profit**. The profit can go to the owners of the business, to the people who work there or to make the business bigger.

There are two kinds of business:

One makes things to sell. It is called a business which produces **goods**.

The other does things for people. It is called a business which offers **services**.

Some businesses do both. A car manufacturer may make, sell and service cars.

Most businesses **compete** with one another. The customers can choose where they buy things, what they buy and who they ask to do things for them. To attract customers, a business needs to stand out from the competition. To do this it needs its own look or **image**. A bank needs a serious image, a toy shop needs a fun image.

A business creates its own image in many different ways.

The name

'The Double-Dough Cake Company'.

The name says something about the work which the business does, where it is or the people working in it.

The logo

A logo is a small picture or symbol which gives people an easy way of recognizing the business. It is a kind of shorthand version of the name.

The notepaper

Often one of the first things you receive from a business is a letter. The notepaper and the things that are written on it are very important ways of attracting customers.

The slogan

'So good you'll want two'.

This is a catchphrase to help advertise the business.

The products

These are the things which the business produces. After they are made, the products need to be packaged to protect them. The packaging can be used to advertise the product.

The premises

This is where the business is based. Customers often visit the premises. Where these are can make a big difference to the image of the business.

The workforce

People make the business work. A good business looks after its workforce. They may be given uniforms or protective clothing, special training and other privileges.

The vehicles

Vehicles can be an advertisement for the business. The way they are painted, looked after and driven can say a lot about the business.

HOW TO DO GOOD BUSINESS

The market price

People may like what you are offering but they may not be able to afford your prices. The highest price you can get is called the **market price**.

You have to ask a price which will cover all your costs and leave you with some profit. Work it out carefully. A production line is where a lot of the same things are made at once. This makes each thing cheaper to make. If you have a production line make sure you can sell everything. It can be expensive to have unsold stocks.

Market research

Finding out what people really want is called **market research**.

It is no good making things to sell if you are the only one who likes them. A **survey** is the best way of doing market research. Ask people a range of questions about your plans and proposals before spending time, effort and money on something no-one wants.

How to do good business

▶ Make sure people want your goods or services.

▶ Make sure people want to pay your prices.

▶ Make sure people know about the business.

▶ Make sure you get the best from your workforce.

▶ Make sure you can deliver the goods and services you are offering.

The business plan

At the start of this book you saw how to organize your work. Businesses have to do the same thing. They use a **business plan**. The plan tells them what they need, when they need it, who does what, how the cash is organized and everything else connected with the business.

Advertising

People will only buy your goods and services if they know about them. You can let people know by **advertising**. Advertisements have to reach the right people. Kids will not be interested in special deals for old age pensioners. Aiming advertisements at the right people . is called **targeting customers**. Advertisements must be honest and fair. Is this always the case?

The workforce

The workers are the most important part of the business. Their pay and their conditions, their health and safety and their training are all the responsibility of the work manager. Make the most of the skills and interests of your workforce. A happy workforce makes a happy business.

MAKING THINGS THAT LOOK GOOD

People have different ideas about beauty. What one person likes, another person might dislike. We judge beauty with our senses. The way things look, smell, feel, sound or taste can all be beautiful. So can the way that people or things move.

Designers should create things which add to the beauty of the world. Here are some guidelines which will help you to produce appealing designs.

Think about these points when you are designing. They all affect the final appearance of the design.

▶ Shape.
▶ Proportion.
▶ Color.
▶ Material.
▶ Texture.
▶ Balance.

Shape

Think about the shape of your object as well as the shapes of the different parts within it.

Many designs use geometric shapes which can be constructed from straight lines and measured angles. Symmetrical shapes can be used to build patterns. Geometrical shapes are often easiest to manufacture. Objects made from geometric shapes look as if they have been built to do a job. We call them **functional**.

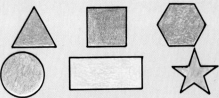

Many shapes can be found in nature and copied for design ideas. Lines in nature tend to flow and look softer than geometric shapes.

Proportion

A heavy table top on tiny legs would look silly. It would be out of proportion. Try to make sure that the sizes of the different parts work well together when you design things.

Material

Would you like eating your breakfast with an iron spoon? It would feel heavy and taste odd. It would probably look a bit rusty as well. There is quite a different 'feel' to artificial materials like plastic compared to natural materials like wood. Think about the properties of the materials which you choose for your designs. The most attractive material may be too expensive or unavailable. In this case you will have to decide on the best alternative.

Texture

The texture on the surface of the material affects both the feel and the look of an object. A smooth surface will reflect light. A rough surface will be dull. The texture can be changed by applying a finish onto the material.

Color

Choosing the right color or combination of colors makes a big difference. Changing one color can completely change the character of something. Would you like grey corn flakes?

Fashion

People's idea about what is good and beautiful can change. Businesses take advantage of this and create new fashions. Fashions in house interiors, cars, music and clothes can change very quickly especially in areas where people have a lot of money to spend. Designers must think about fashion when creating things. Yesterday's designs may not be too popular.

Suitability

Things should be designed for the right places and for the right time. A bright jacket would be right for ski slopes but wrong for birdwatching. Overalls would look a bit silly at a wedding.

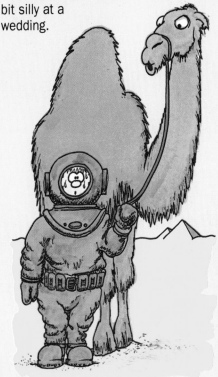

Quality

It is important that things are put together well. A pair of shoes may look beautiful, but they are useless if they fall to bits as soon as they are used. Paying attention to details, making things carefully, with the right materials will give you good results. Always aim for quality.

Fit for human beings

Always think about the needs of humans when you are designing. The size, color and shape of your designs have an affect on the way that your designs will be used. In the Second World War many pilots crashed their planes trying to land. The controls were so similar that tired pilots kept pulling the wrong levers. Changing the designs of the controls made them easier to use. There were fewer accidents because it was harder for pilots to make mistakes.

Think about the size and age of the people who are going to use the things that you design. Things made for young children should be smaller than things made for adults.

FINDING INFORMATION

Writing letters

Writing a letter to a person or a business can bring you a wealth of detailed information. Always explain very clearly what it is you are after. Remember that you are expecting someone to spend time writing back to you so be friendly and explain who you are and why you need the information. If you want to be sure of a reply it is a good idea to enclose a stamped addressed envelope.

Stores

When you are designing something it is useful to see what is already available. Look in stores to see what they are selling, to examine things and to see how much they cost. It is a good idea to tell someone in the store what you are doing and to ask if they mind. Often they will be very helpful and may offer you some leaflets or advice.

Newspapers

Newspapers bring you up to the minute news. They are useful for local and world news. Most libraries keep back numbers of newspapers. This is a good way of finding out about things from the past.

Computer networks

Many businesses and organizations have information stored in databanks. You can reach these if you have a **modem**, which is a telephone connection to a computer. You will also need a phone number and the password which will get you into the databank. Information obtained in this way can be expensive.

Interviewing people

There are experts who can give you just the kind of help that you need. Talking to people can give you another point of view and show you another side of the problem. Always work out your questions and write them down before the interview. A tape player can be a useful way of recording an interview to help you later, but always ask permission first.

Brainstorming

This is a quick way of finding out what you and others think about a subject. Write down everything you can think of to do with the subject.

Other ideas

Visits Nothing compares with first hand experience so arrange a visit and see for yourself.

Exhibitions Look in your local press or library and see if there are any relevant exhibitions in your area. Don't forget permanent exhibitions in museums.

Catalogs When you can't get out to the stores, look through mail order catalogs. You'll find them useful for comparing products and prices.

Books

There is a lot of information in this book so think how much information there must be in a library! Librarians are very helpful people. If you ask politely they are only too pleased to help you to find the books you need. Reference libraries have other information apart from books.

Magazines

There are magazines on every subject you can think of. Many of these are available in the library for you to borrow. Magazines will give you the names of people you can contact for more information.

Using the telephone

For instant answers you cannot beat the telephone. It is often easier to talk to someone on the telephone than face to face. Make sure you know what you are going to say before dialling. Always be polite and speak clearly. Tell people who you are and be friendly.

Television

If you are working on a particular topic then look through the *TV GUIDE* to see if there are any useful programs. Interesting programs come on at the strangest times of the day so check carefully. Some libraries lend out videos on specific subjects. If you can find a TV with teletext you can access a whole stack of up-to-date information.

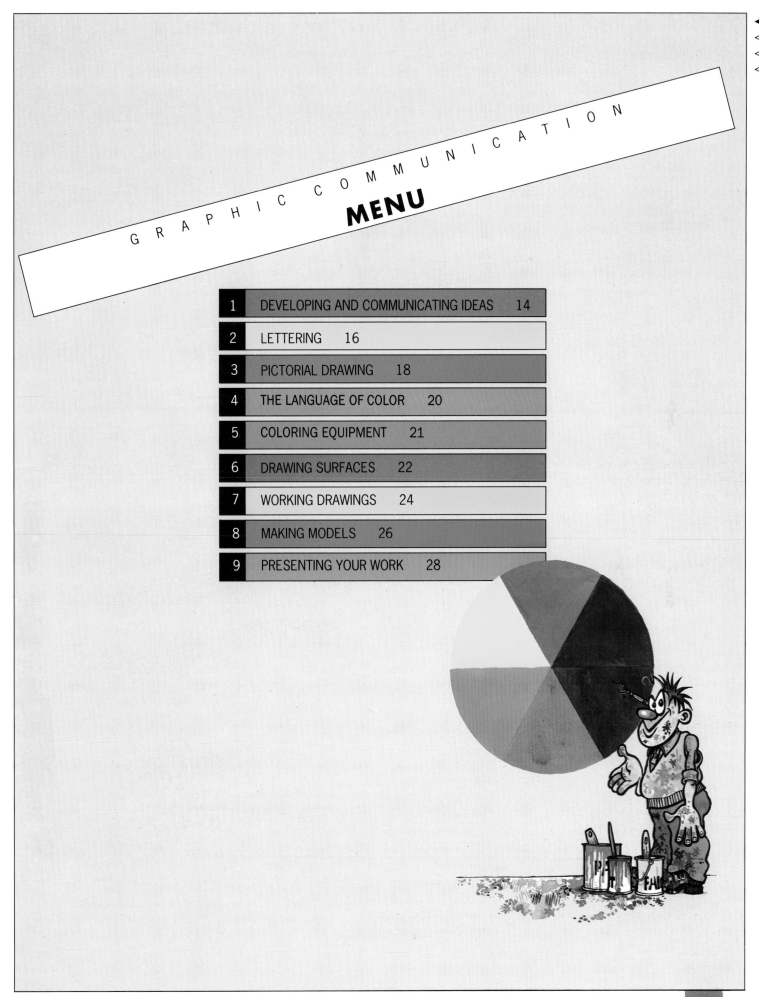

GRAPHIC COMMUNICATION

MENU

1 DEVELOPING AND COMMUNICATING IDEAS

A designer's job is to work out the best way of doing or making something. Designers will some first ideas but these have to be improved or developed.

Of course their ideas are no good locked away in their heads. They have to explain their ideas to other people. This is called communicating design ideas.

There are many ways that designers develop and communicate their ideas. Sometimes designers will use several methods in one project. Here are some ways that you could use:

▶ Sketches

Sketches are simple drawings which explain the basic idea. They might include some useful notes and a little bit of color. Sketches are a quick way of sorting out your different ideas. This is especially useful at the beginning of a project.

▶ Scale drawings

Scale drawings are very carefully drawn plans of objects. They show all the sizes, the materials and the way they are joined together. It is only worth making a scale drawing once you are absolutely clear about the product you are designing.

▶ Storyboards

Storyboards are a series of pictures and words which explain a sequence of events. They work rather like a cartoon strip. You might use storyboards to design a system like a production line or an animation.

▶ Models

Sometimes it is hard to work out or explain an idea by drawing it. It may be easier to make a simple model or a mock-up. A few notes might help your explanation.

In this section you will find different ways to help you to develop and present your design proposals. Whichever way you use, make sure that you keep all your sketches, drawings and models for your final presentation.

Drawing equipment

Graphic communication is a way of using drawings to express yourself. There is a wide range of drawing materials and methods to help you develop and present your ideas.

Paper

Paper comes in different thicknesses or weights, with different surfaces and degrees of transparency.

Detail paper Semi-transparent, thin and white. Used for working out ideas. Grids and drawings will show through.

Cartridge paper Thick, slightly textured surface. Used for finished drawings.

Grid paper Standard grids are helpful when drawing without instruments.

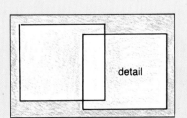
detail

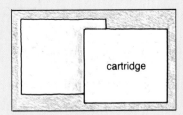
cartridge

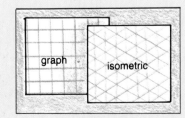
graph   isometric

Pencils

Pencils are graded according to the hardness of the lead.

Soft pencils Range from B to 6B. These are good for shading. 2B is the most useful.

Hard pencils Range from H to 6H. These are good for sharp clear lines. Use 2H for drawing on tracing paper and for lining-in finished drawings. HB is an average general purpose pencil.

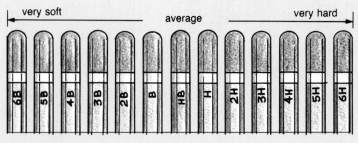
very soft ← | average | → very hard
6B 5B 4B 3B 2B B HB H 2H 3H 4H 5H 6H

SKILL TIP

Mechanical pencils will keep a constant point and stop you from pressing too firmly.

Erasers

There are soft or hard erasers to suit particular needs. A **putty eraser** is used to remove light pencil marks from finished drawings without damaging the paper.

SKILL TIP

Keep erasers clean and hold the paper firmly when erasing.

Rulers

Rules need to have a good straight edge and a clear millimetre scale. Generally a **transparent** ruler is the easiest to use.

SKILL TIP

Mark a measured distance with a **very** short straight line away from the ruler.

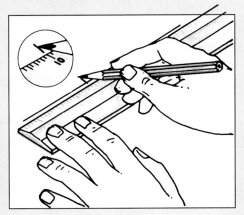

Compasses

A **spring bow compass** is best for drawing accurate circles. Once set, the distance between the pin and the lead will not move.

SKILL TIP

For very small circles use a circle **template** or **stencil**.

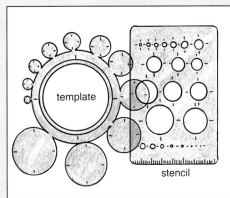

The drawing board

Accurate drawings must be done on a drawing board. The board should be flat and smooth with good straight edges so you can line your work up properly.

SKILL TIP

Line the paper on the board and fix it to the board using masking tape or clips. Do not use scotch tape as this will tear the paper when you try to remove it.

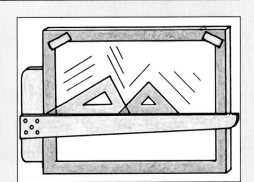

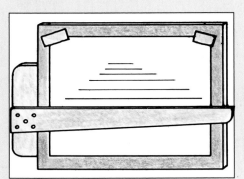

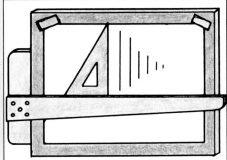

Horizontal lines are drawn with a T-square or a parallel motion straight-edge.

Vertical lines are drawn using a triangle together with the T-square.

Standard triangles are used to draw 30, 60 and 45 degree lines. Other angles can be drawn using an adjustable square.

Lettering is much more than simply writing down words. It is a way of **communicating** with people.

Lettering can be a very powerful tool. It can inform, impress, deceive, amuse and annoy.

Lettering techniques

There are many different alphabet styles called **fonts**. Fonts come in different sizes which are measured in **points**. This lettering is done in News Gothic and is 10 point size.

This is 6 point Goudy

This is 8 point Avant Garde

This is 10 point Courier

This is 12 point Century Schoolbook

This is 14 point Garamond

This is 18 point Bembo

This is 20 point Futura

This is 22 point Helvetica

This is 24 point Times

This is 26 point Palatino

This is 28 point Times Italic

This is 30 point Gill

Freehand

Freehand lettering is special because it is very individual. It is easiest to write in capitals. Use parallel guidelines to keep the heights of letters constant. Measure 3, 5 or 7 mm gaps between the guidelines.

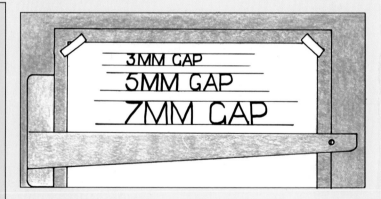

Stencils

Stencils come in limited styles but in a range of sizes. Stencils have engraved guidelines which you must line up over your own pencil guideline. You can fill in the missing parts of the letters or leave the stencil effect.

SKILL TIPS

To produce good lettering:

1 **Always** draw guide lines to keep letters straight. Guide lines help to produce special effects.

2 Count the letters, measure the space vertically and horizontally and work out what size letters will fit. Allow for gaps between words.

3 Map out your lettering lightly in pencil before committing yourself in ink.

Dry transfers

Sheets of dry transfer lettering come in many different sizes, styles and colors.

To use:

1 Remove the backing paper. The sheets have guidelines which you must line up with your own pencil guideline.

2 Transfer the letters by rubbing over them with a pencil.

3 If you are happy with their position then fix them permanently by rubbing again through the backing paper. This is called **burnishing**.

4 Always protect the sheets by storing them with the backing paper.

SKILL TIP

Use the lines and other symbols which are on the dry transfer sheets.

Computer generated print

With appropriate software you can design your own lettering on a computer and print the result on a variety of paper. This is especially useful when you need to use a lot of lettering.

Wordprocessing packages give access to a wide range of font styles and sizes. You can also create many special effects.

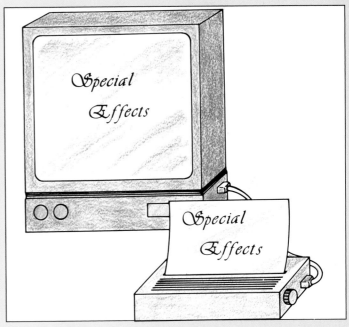

Photocopier

You can use a photocopier to enlarge or reduce your lettering. A good photocopy often looks better than the original. Cutting and pasting your photographs gives you the opportunity to try different layouts.

3 PICTORIAL DRAWING

Designers use a **pictorial drawing** to show more than one side of an object at a time. Drawing three-dimensional views can be helpful when working out ideas.

All objects can be represented as rectangular box shapes.

Drawing objects by fitting them inside rectangular boxes is called **crating**.

In order to show three sides of the object, the box is drawn at an angle.

Isometric drawings

If two sides of an object are drawn at angles of 30 degrees to the horizontal the result is an **isometric** drawing.

Isometric drawing can be done with isometric grid paper or drawing instruments.

Isometric grid paper

Isometric grid paper consists of three sets of parallel lines running at 60 degrees to one another. From any point where the lines cross there are three axes which define the three dimensions, **depth**, **length** and **height**.

Height is measured on the vertical axis. Length and depth are measured on the other two axes.

Follow the grid lines to define the **plan** (top), **end** (side) and **front** views of your drawing.

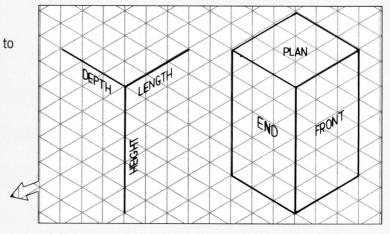

SKILL TIP

1   Clip detail paper over the grid paper and trace over it.

2   Alternatively, draw on the grid paper itself and make a photocopy. You will lose the blue grid lines which will not be reproduced.

Drawing instruments will help you to draw your own isometric grid lines.

You will need the 30/60 degree triangle.

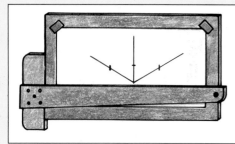
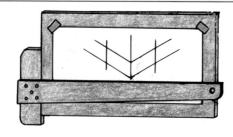
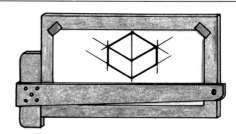

1   Draw a vertical line.
2   Draw two 30 degree lines crossing at a point on the vertical.
3   Measure and mark the length, depth and height from this point.

4   Draw two 30 degree lines from the height mark. Draw vertical lines from the length and depth marks.

5   Draw 30 degree lines in from the top corners.

Once you have the right shaped crate you can draw in the object.

Oblique drawings

When one side of an object is drawn straight on and the other sides are drawn at angles of 45 degrees to the first side then the result is called an **oblique** drawing.

Oblique drawings are especially useful when designing complicated shapes.

Isometric tubes, cylinders and cones

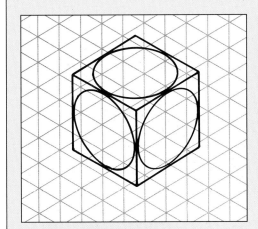

In isometric drawings, circles appear as **ellipses**. An ellipse is a squashed circle. It has two axes. The long axis is the true diameter of the circle. The short axis always lies along a grid line. Ellipse stencils with engraved axes can be a great help.

SKILL TIPS

1 Use pencil shading to give your drawings more of a three-dimensional feel.

2 Vary the weight and the direction of the shading for each view.

3 Shade the cylinders along the edges, fading in towards the front of the drawing.

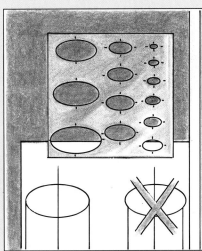

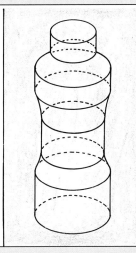
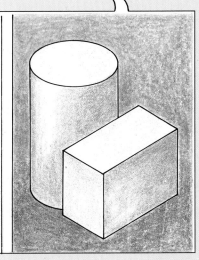

1 Draw an ellipse on a center line.

2 Draw two sides down from the edges of the ellipse. Measure the height.

3 Draw another ellipse between the sides for the base.

4 Any lettering must go around the cylinder on elliptical guidelines.

5 You can combine various sizes of ellipse to create more complex designs.

Color – the basics

There are three **primary** colors: **red**, **blue** and **yellow**.

Mixing two primary colors gives a **secondary** color. The three secondary colors are:

Complimentary colors go well together. They are neighbors in the color wheel.

Contrasting colors clash with each other. They are opposite each other in the color wheel.

Every color has a range of **tones** from very light to very dark. Adding black to a color makes a **shade**. Adding white to a color makes a **tint**.

Pure colors and all their tones have a standard **value**. This makes its possible to match and coordinate any color.

MAKE COLOR WORK FOR YOU

Color has a great effect on the way we see and feel about things. Choose color carefully in your designs.

Color coding – general rules

Black	Mysterious, heavy
White	Clean, pure
Yellow	Warm, friendly, happy
Red	Hot, dangerous
Blue	Cool, clear, sad
Green	Relaxing, fresh
Brown	Natural, earthy
Gold and silver	Rare, expensive
Primary colors	Bright, fun
Pastel colors	Calm, subdued

SKILL TIPS

1 Keep color combinations simple.

2 Use several colors with the same tone or several tones of one color.

3 Contrast small amounts of one color with its opposite.

4 Use roughly equal areas of complimentary colors.

Coloring tools

Different coloring tools can be used to produce different results.

Crayons are cheap, come in a wide range of colors and are easy to use.

Pastels produce soft colors and are good for coloring large areas. They can be messy if not used with care. Pastels are available as chalk sticks or crayons.

Markers are available in a wide variety of point sizes, inks and colors. It is almost impossible to correct mistakes once you have made a mark.

SKILL TIPS

1 For drawing use the end of the crayon.
2 For shading use the side of the crayon.
3 To show flat surfaces shade in one direction.
4 For a neat edge shade up against the edge of a ruler.
5 Sharpen an edge by lining it in.
6 Soften an edge by leaving a gap between adjoining surfaces.

SKILL TIPS

1 Scrape a pile of powder off the stick and spread it with a cotton wool pad. Protect areas which you want to keep clean with a piece of card.
2 You can mix or fade colors.
3 You can add details and sharpen edges with pastel crayons.
4 Try using pastels on colored paper. It can produce effective results.
5 Spray your pastel drawings with a fixative to stop them from smudging.

SKILL TIPS

1 Do not press too hard and damage the point.
2 Do not scrub the paper with the pen tip.
3 Color wide areas by drawing a series of parallel lines with a chisel point pen.
4 Use thin points for details and lining in.
5 Markers can bleed through paper so only use one side.

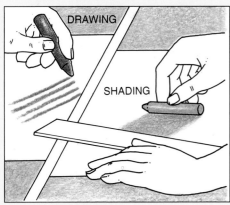

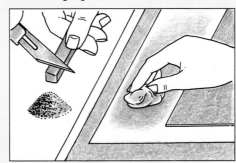

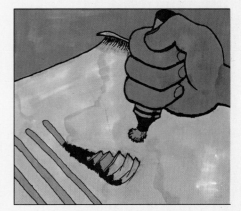

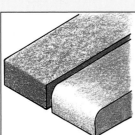

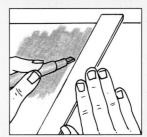

You can make your drawings come to life by dressing them with appropriate surfaces.

Decide upon the material, color and surface texture that you want.

Select from the list below the surface which most closely matches the one you want to create. Use the recommended tools and techniques.

Creating textures

Dull/shiny Dull surfaces should be plain. Draw reflections to show a shiny surface. Two or three streaks of light or dark will do. Increase the contrast to turn on the shine.

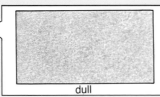
dull

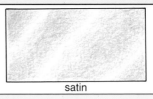
satin

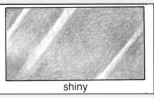
shiny

Creating materials

Natural wood

Main features: grain patterns, variable color, warm texture.

Use yellow, orange and brown crayons.

1 Draw grain line with a sharp brown crayon. Grain lines never cross. They always meet at edges.

2 Shade lightly with a mixture of yellow, orange and brown crayons, depending on the color and type of wood. Always shade in the direction of the grain pattern.

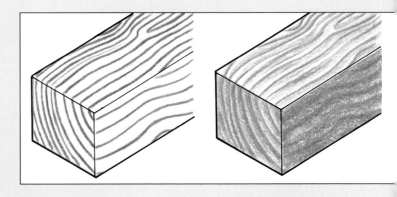

Metals

Main features: hard, smooth surface with consistent color.

Use crayons, pastels or markers.

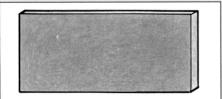

Steel Even grey shading.

Aluminium Even silvery grey shading. Give aluminium a hint of grain and a slight shine.

Copper/brass Orange or browny orange.
Shade evenly over the whole surface.

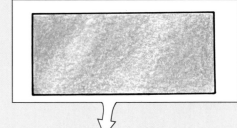

Chrome Use a high contrast combination of black and white to show reflections.

Acrylic

Main features: consistent colors, usually smooth and shiny with no grain.

Use markers for shiny surfaces, pastels for dull surfaces.

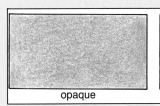

opaque   semi-transparent   transparent

Clear/opaque Opaque materials block out the background. Draw in clearer details as the material becomes more transparent.

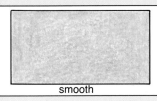
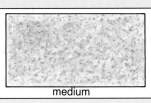
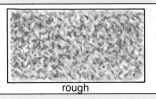

smooth   medium   rough

Rough/smooth Color evenly for smooth materials. Use small marks with different directions, sizes and styles to show different types of texture.

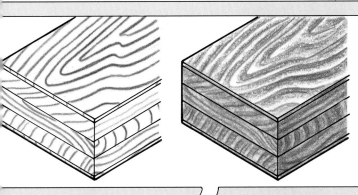
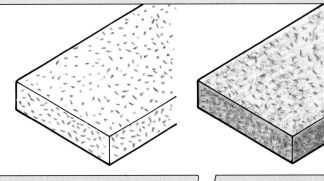

Plywood

Main features: wood surface, sandwich pattern on edges.

Use yellow, orange and brown crayons.

1 Draw the top wooden surface.

2 Draw the strips of veneer along the edges.

3 Color alternate strips with light, long-grain patterns and dark, short-grain patterns. Remember to reverse the order on adjoining strips.

Partical Board

Main features: no grain but a wooden texture.

Use creamy yellow crayons.

1 Cover the area with a series of short random marks.

2 Color the surface a creamy yellow.

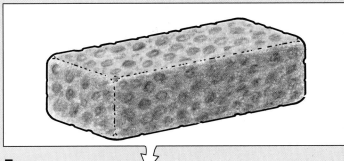

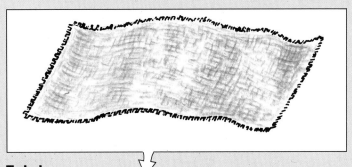

Foam

Main features: spongy, soft, slightly rough texture.

Use circular texture marks and pastels or markers.

Fabric

Main features: weave, softness and floppiness.

Use slightly squiggly lines close together in two directions. Color with crayons.

Working drawings explain how things will look and how they will be made. There are set ways of showing this information. Learn the rules so that you will be able to 'read' other people's drawings and so that they will be able to read yours.

All drawings should have:

► The title
► Your name
► The units of measurement
► The scale used
► A neat border.

Setting out your drawing

A **first angle orthographic projection** is an accurate drawing which shows all the views and includes every detail and measurement.

Arranging the views

The three views, **front**, **end** and **plan**, are drawn straight on and arranged so that the common dimensions line up.

It is worth making a rough sketch to see how the views will fit on your paper. The front view is always placed at the top left hand part of the paper.

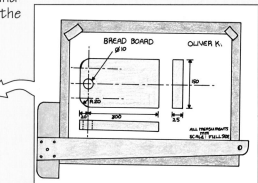

SKILL TIPS

You will have to line in the finished work to show the outlines. You must erase out all the unwanted lines at the end so draw all your construction lines faintly.

Draw the front view first. Use a 45 degree line from the bottom right hand corner of the front view. Draw the end view and transfer dimensions for the plan view using this line.

Add the details after you have drawn the outlines of the main views.

Dimensioning

It is important to show all the dimensions on your drawing.
Use **dimension lines** and sharp arrows to show distances.
Use the symbol R for radius and ϕ for diameter.
Use **center lines** to show centers.
Full size drawings are usually done in millimeters.
Whatever the scale, always show the measurements as their true value.

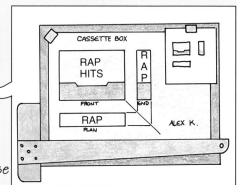

Scale

It is not possible to draw everything full sized. Some things need to be drawn larger in order to see the details more clearly. Some need to be drawn smaller in order to fit on the paper.

In scale drawings, all the dimensions are increased or decreased by the same degree.

Useful scales

Notation	All dimensions
10:1	x 10
2:1	x 2
1:1	full size
1:2	x 1/2
1:10	x 1/10
1:50	x 1/50

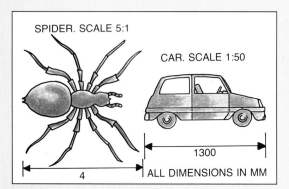

SPIDER. SCALE 5:1

CAR. SCALE 1:50

1300

4

ALL DIMENSIONS IN MM

Hidden detail

Use **dotted lines** to show what is going on behind, inside or through an object. Keep the dashes and spaces equal in size for a neat appearance.

Cross-sections

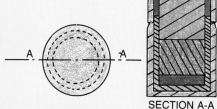

SECTION A-A

Exploded views

An exploded view is a good way of showing the parts of an object and how they fit together.

1 Start by making an isometric drawing of the main part.

2 Then draw the components spreading them out along their isometric axes. Keep the parts in the right order and along the correct axes.

One way of showing the inside of an object is to cut it straight across and draw the **sectional view**.

Mark the section clearly on your main drawing. Cross-hatch the solid part of the section.

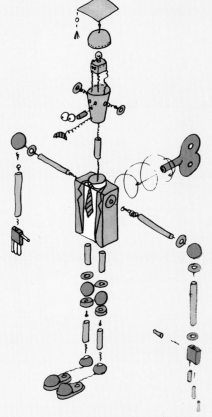

Enlarged views

A small part of your drawing may need to be explained in greater detail. You can do this using words or by drawing an enlarged view. Be sure to show clearly which part you are enlarging.

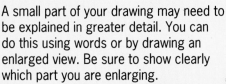

DETAIL: KNOBBLY KNEE

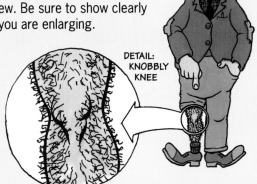

Movement

To show how your design will move you can:

1 Use arrows.

2 Use words.

3 Draw ghost pictures.

4 Draw several pictures.

HAMMER HITS HEAD HERE

Model making is an important part of the design process, and can save time, patience and money. It can help you to get the size of things right, to work out details and to present your proposals effectively.

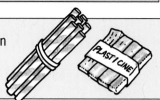

Types of models

Card models

Many objects can be made by folding card. A **surface development** or net of the object can be drawn onto card, cut out, scored, folded and glued. Include any graphic designs on the development before cutting out the net. Standard nets can be adapted to make different models.

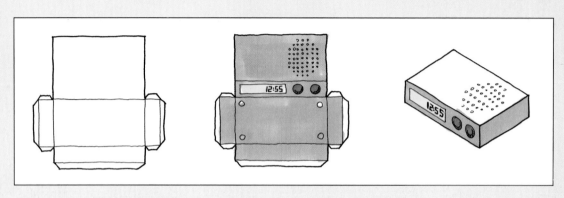

CRATE	DEVELOPMENT	DETAILS AND TABS	SCORED, CUT FOLDED AND GLUED
			DICE
			BUS
		MUG	MUG
			HAT
			PYRAMID

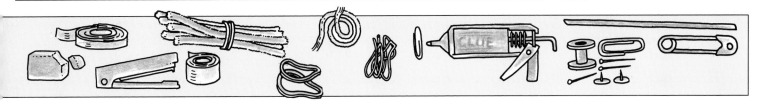

Solid models

Make a solid model if it needs extra strength or has detailed edges and surfaces.

Balsa, or styrofoam are easy-to-work modeling mediums. Draw the views on each side of a rectangular block of modeling material. Shade the waste material. Work on one view at a time. Use a small saw, files, and abrasive paper. Take care to **avoid dust** especially when using styrofoam. Color models with poster paints.

SKILL TIP

Mix the paint with a little white glue to add a slight shine.

Frame models

Mock-ups of structures can be made using card and small section timber. Measure lengths and the position of joints carefully. Use quick-drying glue or a glue gun to make the joint stick.

Construction kits

Lego, Fischer-Technik and Meccano are three types of construction kits which can help you to explore and understand ideas and concepts.

Other aids to modelling

Any of these may be useful for your model:

- ▶ Stapler
- ▶ Scotch tape
- ▶ Blu-tak
- ▶ Rubber bands
- ▶ Glue gun
- ▶ Wire
- ▶ Welding rod
- ▶ Paper clips
- ▶ Pins
- ▶ String
- ▶ Straws
- ▶ Plasticine
- ▶ Pipe cleaners
- ▶ Cotton reels.

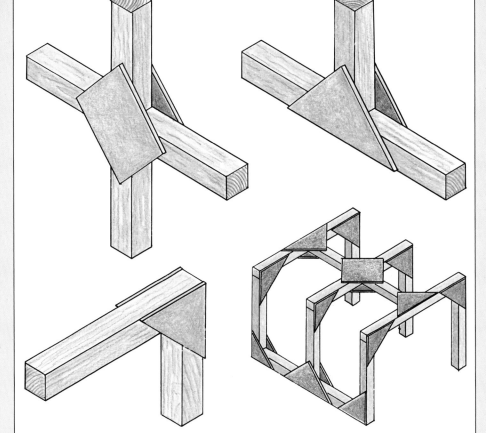

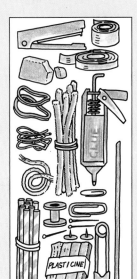

9 PRESENTING YOUR WORK

Make the best of your work by presenting it well. The way you present your work tells people something about you.

General points

▶ Keep all your work from the very first design idea to your final presentation drawing.

▶ Use a stiff folder to carry your work around. This way, it will stay flat and clean.

▶ Title and name every piece of work that you do.

SKILL TIP

1 Mount work straight and level on stiff paper or card. Use gluesticks or spraymount, not white glue which will spoil the paper.

2 Vary the size and contrast of your borders.

3 Draw frames around your drawings with crayons or markers. Take care, or you could ruin important work!

4 Mount your work in interesting ways to achieve special effects.

5 Relate your models to your drawings using color, position and suitable backgrounds.

S Y S T E M S
MENU

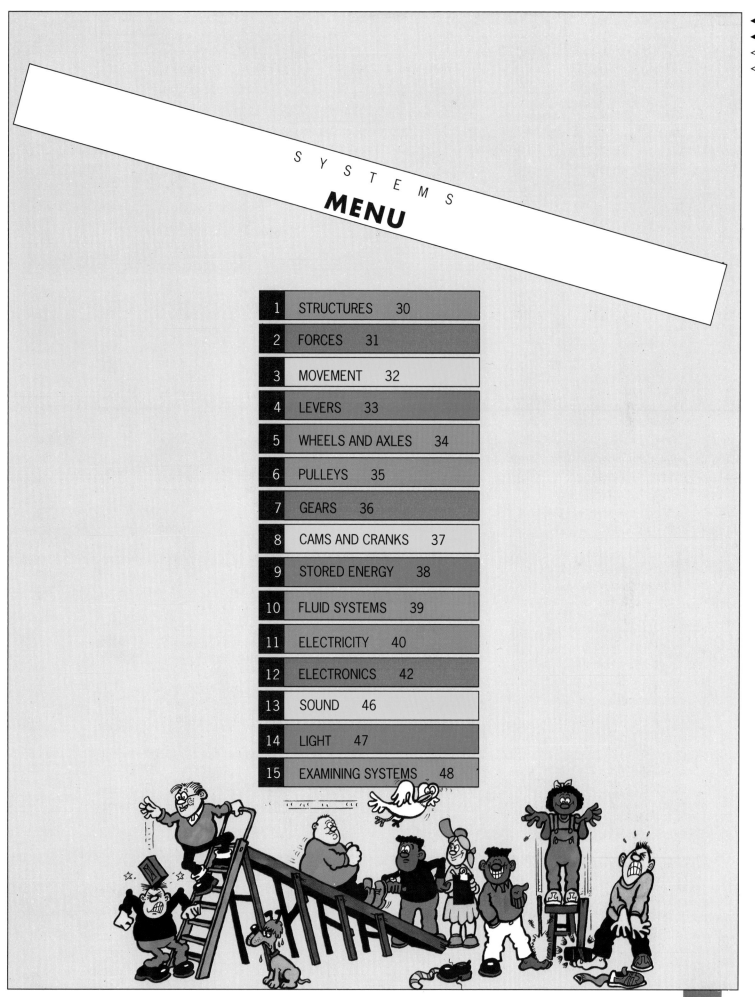

A **structure** is something built from separate parts which have been joined together.

Structures need to be able to survive in their intended environment and support any expected loads. Designers study different kinds of structures and the forces which try to destroy them in order to find the most suitable materials and methods of construction.

Shapes can be strengthened using triangulation.

Building structures

Structures can be **rigid** or **flexible**. For example, a tire is flexible but a wheel is rigid.

Structures can be **frames** or **shells**. For example, a gate is a frame but a door is a shell. In practice most structures are a combination of shell and frame structures.

Stability

Everything on earth is being pulled towards the center of the earth by the force of **gravity**. The greater the **mass** of an object, the stronger the pull of gravity will be and the heavier it will feel. In fact, gravity only acts on one point of an object. This is called the **center of mass** or the **center of gravity**. Imagine a line between the center of the earth and the center of gravity. An object is **stable** if this line passes through its base. Otherwise it is unstable and it will fall over.

Three things affect the stability of an object.

1 **The size of the base.** The larger the base, the more stable the object.

2 **The position of the center of gravity.** The lower the center of gravity, the more stable the object.

3 **The angle of the base.** The object becomes less stable as the angle between the base and the horizontal increases.

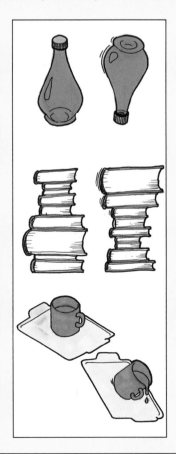

Strength

Structures need to be strong enough to resist destructive forces. The shape of a structure, the type of materials used and the way they are put together all contribute towards the strength of an object. Structures are subjected to different types of forces which produce different kinds of destruction.

Breaking strain is the amount of force a structure can take before it collapses.

Elasticity measures the amount of deformity an object can take under strain and still return to its original shape when the force is released.

1 Compression – crushing

Use materials in the most suitable direction.

Tubes will crush one way but not the other.

2 Tension – snapping

An object being stretched is under **tension**. Tension increases rigidity.

Bending is a combination of compression and tension.

3 Torsion – twisting

When an object is twisted it is under torsion. Torsion occurs along the **length** of the object being twisted.

4 Shear – cutting

A shearing force occurs when one layer of material tries to slide over a parallel layer.

Types of movement

Movement in a straight line

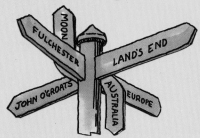

The direction of a movement can be related to three axes:

◀ up/down

◀ left/right

◀ forwards/backwards.

Going backwards and forwards in a straight line in any direction is called a **reciprocating movement**. A saw uses this type of movement.

Circular movement

Rotational movement can be clockwise or counter-clockwise.

Swinging backwards and forwards about a point is called an **oscillating movement**. A pendulum uses this type of movement.

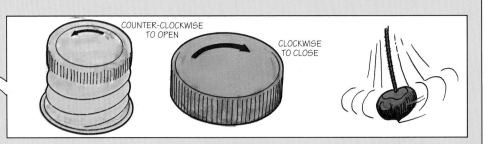

Machines

Machines work by using a form of energy (an input) and converting it into an action (an output).

Power measures the amount of mechanical energy that a machine supplies.

Efficiency Energy is **lost** in the actual operation of a machine. The more **efficient** a machine is, the less energy is lost in this way.

Mechanisms control the way a machine moves. Different mechanisms will give quite different outputs for the same energy input.

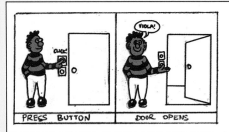

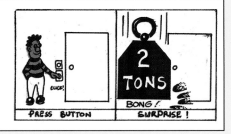

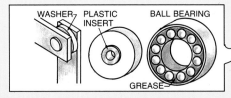

Friction is the grip between two surfaces. It stops things from slipping. Friction can be useful or it can be a problem. Friction uses up mechanical energy, making surfaces hot and causing increased wear.

Lubricants are one way to reduce friction. Waxy or oily substances are good lubricants. They form a slippery film between moving surfaces.

Bearings are used to separate the moving parts of a mechanism. Bearings are made from hard-wearing or slippery materials and help the moving parts to last longer.

How levers work

A **lever** is a rigid rod with a turning point called a pivot. Levers can be used to change the **direction** and the **size** of a movement or force.

A **linkage** is a mechanism made from several levers. Standard combinations of levers are used to produce specific types of mechanism.

The three types of lever are:

Class one lever
PIVOT SMALL EFFORT
LARGE LOAD

Class two lever
PIVOT SMALL EFFORT
LARGE LOAD

Class three lever
LARGE EFFORT SMALL LOAD
PIVOT

SMALL DISTANCE LARGE DISTANCE
PAINT

SMALL DISTANCE LARGE DISTANCE

SMALL DISTANCE LARGE DISTANCE

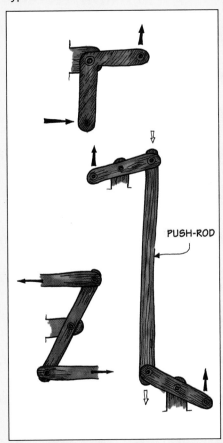

PUSH-ROD

PLYWOOD   DOWEL   METAL STRIP   METAL ROD   FLATTENED ROD   STRING

Building linkages

▲ Experiment with cardboard strips, paper clips and drawing pins to get your linkages right.

▲ Use guides to keep the levers where you want them.

▲ Use cables or string to operate levers by remote control.

▲ Levers can often be disguised.

▲ Levers must move smoothly on their pivots. Make sure that the pivot suits the hole.

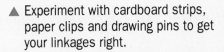
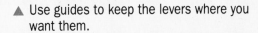
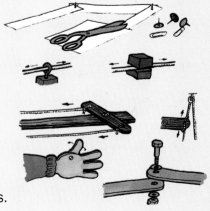

Lever problems – jammed linkages

1 Pivots too tight or too loose.

2 Linkage connected incorrectly.

3 Guides too close together.

CREAK

4 Linkage too long or too short.

5 Linkage out of line.

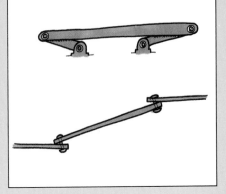

How wheels work

A wheel depends upon **friction** to make it work. An **axle** runs through the center of the wheel.

Wheel systems

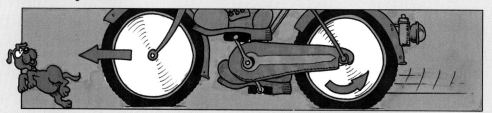

▶ **Free wheel** – the bike moves forward, the tire cannot slip so the wheel turns around.

▶ **Driven wheel** – the axle turns the wheel. The tire cannot slip and so it pushes the bike forward.

Making wheels

There are various ways of making wheels. You can:

▲ Use ready made wheels.

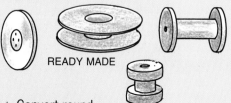

READY MADE

▲ Convert round objects into wheels.

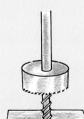

HOLE SAW

▲ Cut a disc with a hole saw.

▲ Cut thick dowel into short sections.

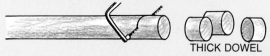

THICK DOWEL

▲ Cut plywood into circular shapes.

▲ Shape pieces of wood into wheels on a lathe.

COPING SAW AND SANDER

LATHE

Keeping wheels on axles

Use:

▶ Plastic or rubber tubing.

▶ A locking peg, pin or clip.

▶ Lock nuts.

▶ Screw and washers.

▶ Axle housings.

KEEPING WHEELS ON AXLES

RUBBER OR PLASTIC TUBING

LOCKING PEG OR PIN

LOCK NUTS

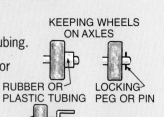

WHEEL FIXED AXLE FREE   WHEEL FREE AXLE FIXED

Wheel problems

1   **Wobbly ride**
Wheel not round, off-center axle, hub too large, hub not square through wheel, bent axle.

2   **Wheels sticky**
Axle too tight, crooked axle makes wheel jam, needs lubrication.

3   **Wheels fall off**
Loose lock nuts, fasteners too slack.

How pulleys work

A **pulley** is a grooved wheel which carries a rope or belt. Friction holds the rope on the pulley which it turns as the rope is pulled.

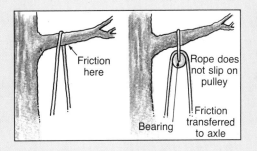

Friction here

Rope does not slip on pulley

Bearing

Friction transferred to axle

SKILL TIPS

1 A good pulley should have an even groove with sides high enough to hold the belt in place.

2 The axle needs to fit well and lie square onto the pulley.

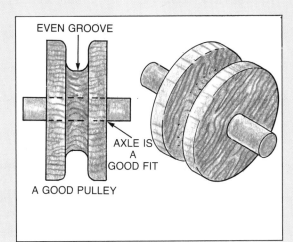

EVEN GROOVE

AXLE IS A GOOD FIT

A GOOD PULLEY

Pulley systems

Pulleys can be used:

▶ To help move or lift things

▶ To change speeds – one turn – lots of turns.

▶ To change direction – twist in belt, two pulleys.

▶ To connect moving systems – conveyors, extensions.

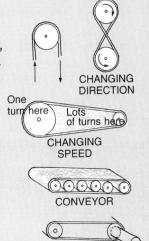

CHANGING DIRECTION

One turn here

Lots of turns here

CHANGING SPEED

CONVEYOR

EXTENSIONS

Making pulleys

You can:

▲ Use ready made pulleys.

▲ Shape pulleys on a lathe.

READY MADE

DOUBLE PULLEY

LATHE

▲ Glue three layers together. Locate the centers with the axle.

3 LAYERS GLUED TOGETHER

LOCATE CENTERS WITH AXLE

Pulley problems

1 **Belt keeps slipping** loose belt.

2 **System jams** belt too tight, axles too tight, requires lubricating.

3 **Belt keeps snapping** belt too thin, mechanism too fast.

4 **Belt falls off** axles out of line, groove crooked or too shallow, axle too loose.

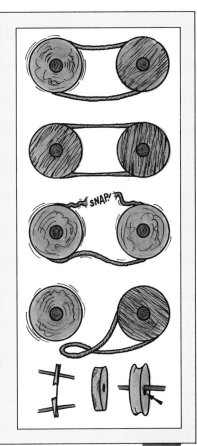

SNAP!

Gear systems

▶ Gears can be used like pulleys. In this case they are connected by chains. The holes in the links must match the teeth of the gears. The chain/gear system gives a more positive connection than the pulley/belt system.

▶ Different sized gears can be connected together to change speeds. These systems are called **geartrains**. The ratio between the number of teeth on one gear the the number of teeth of the next one is called the **gear ratio**. A **gearbox** has several geartrains which can be selected by a gearchange.

▶ A **bevel gear** has teeth cut at an angle of 45 degrees. It meshes with a similar gear. It is used to change the direction of turning through 90 degrees.

▶ A **worm gear** drives a cog and turns the axis of rotation through 90 degrees.

▶ A **rack and pinion gear** converts circular movement to reciprocal movement.

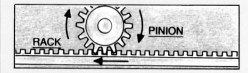

▶ A **rachet mechanism** only allows rotation in one direction.

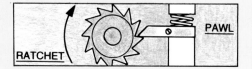

How gears work

Gears or **cogs** are wheels with teeth which are evenly spaced and of the same size. The teeth of one gear connect or **mesh** with the teeth of an adjoining gear. The teeth of both gears must match in size and shape.

Effective gears need to be made accurately since every single tooth must mesh.

▲ Gears are available ready made in nylon or brass. To hold them on the axle they often have a **set screw** which should be tight.

▲ Corrugated paper makes useful gear systems.

▲ A simple bevel gear system can be made using rods sticking out of a solid disc.

Gear problems

1 **Gears keep sticking:**
   chain too tight,
   chain doesn't match teeth,
   axles too tight,
   part of mechanism jamming the system,
   damaged teeth.

2 **Chain keeps falling off:**
   incorrect chain for the teeth,
   gears out of line.

3 **Noisy system:**
   worn teeth,
   loose chain.

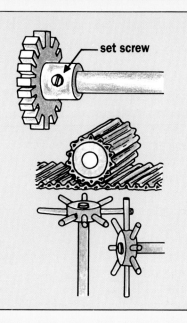

How cams work

A **cam** is a specially shaped wheel which moves a **cam follower** up and down as it rotates.

The **profile** or shape of the cam affects the way that the cam follower moves.

Cam systems

▶ An **eccentric cam** is a wheel fitted off-center. It produces one life of the cam follower per revolution.

▶ A **snail cam** gives a slow lift and a sudden drop. It can only work in one direction.

▶ Cams can be used to make things dip as well as lift.

▶ A cam follower can be a push rod or a lever.

CAM FOLLOWER

ECCENTRIC CAM

SNAIL CAM

Four lifts per rev.
One dip per rev.

Making cams

▲ Decide on the type of movement you want to achieve before designing the cam.

▲ Cam followers need to be in contact with their cams at all times. Use gravity, springs or elastic to do this.

▲ Cut cams from plywood or acrylic sheet. Make sure the axles are a good fit.

SKILL TIP

Avoid sharp corners in your cams.

Cam problems

1 **Cam keeps sticking**
axle not square onto the cam, too tight, system needs lubricating.

2 **Cam follower doesn't move**
guides too tight or in the wrong position.

How cranks work

A crank can change rotary movement into reciprocal movement. A lever called a **connecting rod** or **conrod** is attached to a bent axle. As the axle revolves, the conrod moves up and down. (The conrod can also be connected to the side of a wheel.)

A crank can also work the other way around. If the conrod is moved up and down it will drive a wheel.

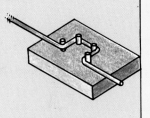

Crank systems

▶ A cranked axle works like a lever. This is useful for handles.

▶ The conrod will move both up and down and side to side. A second lever and a pivot is used to stop the side to side movement.

Making cranks

▲ Use guides to hold connecting rods in position. If you are not using a second pivot you will need to allow space for the side to side movement.

▲ Use a jig to bend the axles. Do not try to bend thick axles.

▲ Make sure you have enough space to slip the connecting rod over the shaft.

Crank problems

1 **Lever keeps jamming**
connection on axle too slack so it slips off guides too close together.

2 **Mechanism sticky**
connection on axle too tight, shaft crooked or out of line.

CRANK

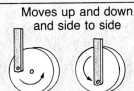
Moves up and down and side to side

Second pivot stops side to side movement

Stored energy systems

The energy needed to move objects can be generated in several different ways.

▶ Potential energy

Gravity ensures that anything which goes up must come down. Objects gain potential energy when they go up. They lose it when they fall down. Potential energy is stored by maintaining height. Potential energy is used by controlling the speed and the direction in which objects drop.

1 When an object drops from a height a lot of energy can be used or wasted on impact.

2 The longer an object takes to fall the less energy is used on impact. Slopes slow down descents.

3 The weight of an object does not affect the speed at which it drops. However, the heavier the object the greater the release of energy will be on impact.

Elastic energy

Elastic materials store energy when they are stretched or compressed. When released, they return to their original shape giving up their store of energy.

A **spring** is an elastic device. There are two types of spring.

1 Compression spring

Tightening the spring stores the energy.

2 Tension spring

Stretching the spring stores the energy.

Rubber

Elastic thread and rubber bands can be stretched to store energy.

SKILL TIPS

1 The thickness and length of a spring or rubber band determines its power.

2 All elastic materials have a tolerance beyond which they will snap.

3 Fix the ends of a spring or band using loops or hooks. The fixing must be stronger than the maximum power of the spring or band.

How fluid systems work

When something is pushed it tries to move. If a line of people is pushed at one end, the movement will spread down the line to the other end. Fluids, which can be gas or liquid, can be pushed in a similar way to make things move. The harder the push, the greater the power of the system.

Hydraulic systems use a liquid. Water only works for low-pressure systems as it is easily 'squashed'. High pressure systems use hydraulic oil.

Pneumatic systems use a gas such as air. The air must be compressed before it can be used. Pneumatic system are cleaner than hydraulic systems but tend to make more noise.

Both systems require an **input** to move the fluid, a **control** to direct the flow and an **output** to use the moving fluid.

Both systems require a reservoir or container to hold the fluid.

Air can be pumped into a sealed tank until it is filled with **compressed air**. This is exactly what happens in a tire. The compressed air can be released from the tank as it is needed.

If a reservoir of water is higher than the output it will be forced through the system by gravity. This is called a gravity-fed system. The higher the reservoir above the output, the greater the pressure at the output.

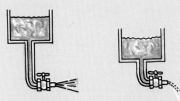

HIGH PRESSURE   LOW PRESSURE

A piston can force fluid from a **master cylinder** into the system. This is how a syringe works.

Control systems

The system needs to be strong enough to cope with the maximum pressure it may need to handle.

Pipes control the direction of flow. The diameter of the pipe is called the **bore**. If the fluid is forced from a wide bore pipe into a narrow bore pipe than the pressure in the system will increase.

Connectors extend the system, alter pressures and direct the flow to different places.

Taps control the amount of fluid which flows through the system.

Valves control the direction of the flow.
Flaps and balls can be used to make valves.

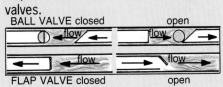

BALL VALVE closed   open

FLAP VALVE closed   open

A **safety valve** operates if the pressure in the system is too high.

Outputs

1 The flow of fluid can push a piston in a **slave cylinder** and activate a mechanical device.

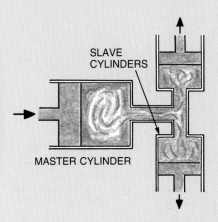

SLAVE CYLINDERS

MASTER CYLINDER

2 Gas or liquid can be released from the system in the form of a jet.

SKILL TIPS

1 Syringes and nylon tubing are useful when building fluid systems. The syringe case needs to be held firmly in place.

2 Use flexible tubing to avoid too many connections.

The electricity supply

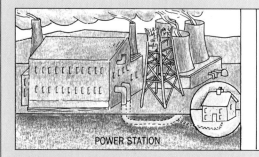

POWER STATION

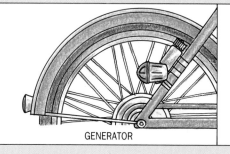

GENERATOR

BATTERY

Electricity is produced on a large scale in power stations. It is fed into a system called the **National Grid**. The grid distributes **mains electricity**. Mains electricity is very powerful and can be very dangerous.

On a smaller scale, electricity can be produced by a **generator** or stored in **batteries**. Generally batteries are a lot safer than mains electricity but they still need to be handled correctly.

Conductors and insulators

Materials which allow electricity to pass through them are called **conductors**. Metals, especially copper, water and people are good conductors.

Materials which do not allow electricity to pass through them are called **insulators**. Plastic, glass and rubber are good insulators.

Circuits

An electric current flows round a **circuit**. The circuit is made up from **components**. All electrical devices have at least two connections or **terminals**.

Current flows from the positive terminal of the battery and back into the negative terminal. Switches and lamps can be connected either way round. Reversing the connections of a motor reverses the direction in which it turns. Some items like buzzers must be connected the right way round.

Red cables are connected to the positive side of the circuit.

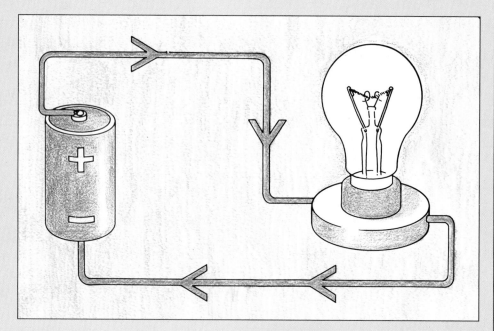

Voltage

The electrical force available is called the **voltage** (v). It is measured in volts. A power station supplies 30 000 volts. Mains supplies 240 volts. A car battery gives 12 volts. High mains voltage can be converted into a low voltage using a **transformer**.

Current

The flow of electric current is measured in **amps**. An electric cooker may use 30 amps. A television may use 1 amp.

A **fuse** protects electrical equipment by stopping too much electrical current passing through. Fuses are rated in amps.

Resistance

Resistors restrict the flow of electricity in a circuit. Resistance is measured in **ohms** or Ω. All electrical components create some resistance. **Variable resistors** can be adjusted. A dimmer switch is controlled by a variable resistor.

Building circuits

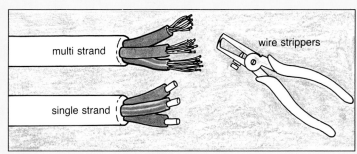

multi strand

wire strippers

single strand

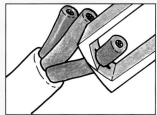

Component	Drawing	Symbol
Battery or supply		
Wire		
Two unconnected wires crossing		
Connected wires		
Lamp		
Motor		
Buzzer		
Slide switch		
Toggle switch		
Push switch		
Reed switch		

Cables

Cables are used to carry electricity.

They are generally made from copper and covered in a PVC sheath. Flexible cables are made from multi-strand copper. Rigid cables are made from a single strand. The thickness of the cable determines the amount of electricity it can carry. Cables are rated in amps.

The insulating sheath is removed from the copper using **wire strippers**. Make sure you use the correct sized notch on the stripper.

An **electrical screwdriver** has an insulated handle.

Connections for joining cables and components can be done using **connecting blocks**, **plugs or sockets**, **crimp connectors**, **alligator clips** or by **soldering**.

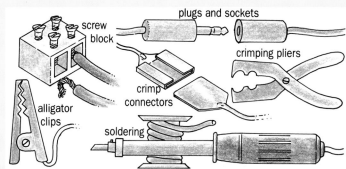

plugs and sockets

screw block

crimping pliers

crimp connectors

alligator clips

soldering

Circuit diagrams

All the parts which make up a circuit can be shown on a **circuit diagram**. Special symbols are used to save drawing all the individual components. The circuit diagram is not an exact drawing of the real circuit but it does show how the components are connected together.

SKILL TIPS

Circuit building

1   First work out your circuit on paper.
2   Collect your components and decide exactly where and how you are going to connect them.
3   Aim to make clean and tidy connections which will be safe and reliable.
4   Check your circuit carefully against your diagram before switching it on.

Electronic systems

Electronic circuits use very small amounts of electric current.

An **input circuit** detects a change in the enviroment. It switches on a **control circuit** which reacts to the change. It activates an **output circuit** which creates a light, sound or movement.

Electronic components

The parts used to build electronic circuits are called **components**. They may include the devices used in electrical circuits in addition to the ones listed below.

Resistors are used to control the flow of electricity in the circuit. The value of the resistors is given by the colored stripes around the resistor. Refer to the chart and read off the value of the resistor. Variable resistors can be used to give a range of values.

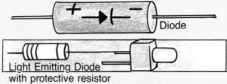

COLOR	1st Band	2nd Band	3rd Band	4th Band	COLOR	1st Band	2nd Band	3rd Band	4th Band
BLACK	0	0	—	TOLERANCE BAND	GREEN	5	5	00000	TOLERANCE BAND
BROWN	1	1	0		BLUE	6	6		
RED	2	2	00		VIOLET	7	7		
ORANGE	3	3	000		GREY	8	8		
YELLOW	4	4	0000		BLACK	9	9		

Electrolytic capacitors can store an electrical charge while the current is flowing. Capacitors are measured in **microfarads** (μF). Their values and maximum operating voltages are marked on them. They must be connected the right way round.

10 μF

A **diode** controls the flow of electricity. It only allows a current to flow in one direction. A **light emitting diode (LED)** gives off light when electricity flows through it. It must be protected by a resistor.

Diode

Light Emitting Diode
with protective resistor

An **NPN transistor** is a sensitive electronic switch. It has three legs: the base, collector and emitter which must all be connected correctly. A resistance is connected to the base leg to protect the transistor from damage.

When the voltage at the base leg is greater than 0.6 volts the transistor will switch on and operate the output circuit.

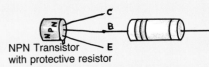

NPN Transistor
with protective resistor

A **microchip** is a miniature control circuit called an **integrated circuit**. It has eight legs which need to be connected correctly.

Microchip

The input circuit

Input circuits have sensors which detect changes.

Input sensors

Light sensor (light dependent resistor) High resistance in the dark, low resistance in the light.

Heat sensor (thermistor) High resistance when cold, low resistance when hot.

Moisture sensor (moisture dependent resistor) High resistance when dry, low resistance when wet.

Control circuits include these devices:

▶ Diode
▶ Transistor
▶ 555 timer chip

Output circuits include these devices:

▶ Loudspeaker
▶ Light emitting diode
▶ Buzzer

Light dependent resistor

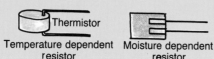

Temperature dependent resistor

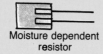

Moisture dependent resistor

COMPONENT	SYMBOL
LDR	
Thermistor	
Moisure Sensor	
Electrolytic Capacitor	
Diode	
NPN Transistor	
555 Microchip	
Loudspeaker	
LED	

Useful circuits

There are standard ways to connect components to achieve particular outputs. A change in resistance in the sensors operates the circuits. The variable resistor allows you to adjust the point at which the device works.

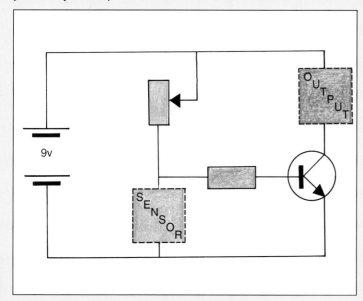

1 Switching on as resistance increases

As the resistance in the sensor increases the input voltage to the transistor also increases. When it rises above 0.6 V it will operate the output device.

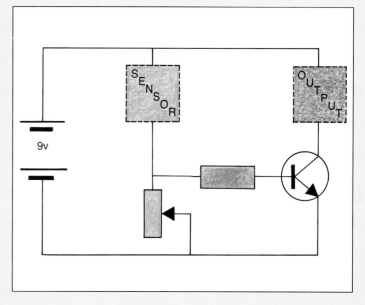

2 Switching on as resistance decreases

As the resistance in the sensor decreases the input voltage to the transistor increases. When it goes above 0.6 V it will operate the output device.

When the circuit is switched on, electricity flows into the capacitor and charges it up. When the voltage rises above 0.6 V the transistor will switch on and operate the output device.

Specific time delays

Use the chart to find out the values of the resistor and the capacitor that you will need for a specific time delay.

1 Use a 1 megaohm variable resistor.
2 Decide upon your required time delay.
3 Select the appropriate capacitor.

Capacitor	Time delay (approx)
100µF	30 secs
220µF	45 secs
470µF	1 min 35 secs
1000µF	4 mins

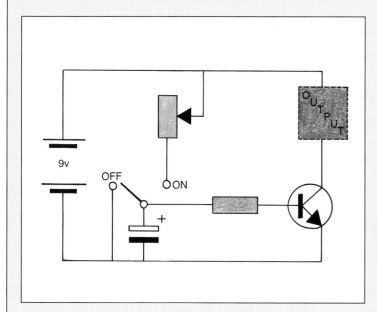

3 Timer circuits

To set a time delay on a switch use a resistor and a capacitor in the input circuit. A variable resistance will allow you to fine-tune the time delay.

Building electronic circuits

Circuit drawings

Before you can build your circuit you have to draw it. Decide what you want each part of your circuit to do. Then draw the circuit plan using the correct symbols. A **component stencil** will help.

Permanent circuits

Breadboards This is a cheap and easy way to build circuits.

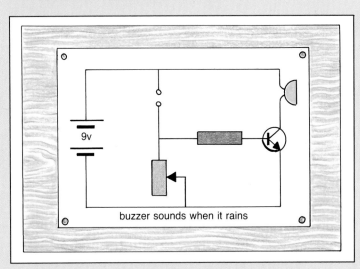

buzzer sounds when it rains

1 Draw a full-size circuit diagram and pin it to a piece of softwood.

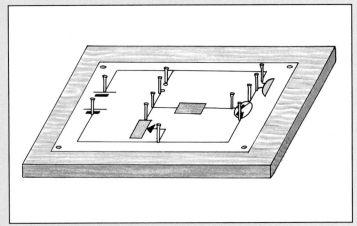

2 Nail panel pins into the board at the points where you will need to make any connections.

Building circuits

SKILL TIPS

1 **Flying leads** are long wires coming out from the main board. They are used to connect external components like batteries.

2 Make your model as similar as you can to your circuit diagram. You are less likely to make mistakes.

3 Avoid squashing the components into too small a space.

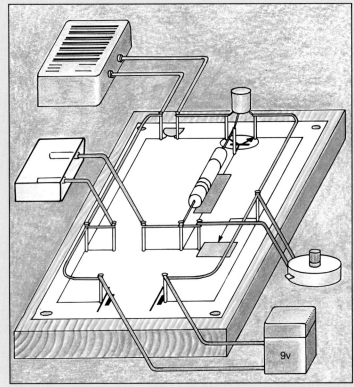

3 Lay out the wires and components matching the diagram and solder them to the pins.

4 Fix external fittings on last using flying leads.

Printed circuits

A **printed circuit board (PCB)** reduces the need for wires between components. It is made from a laminate of a thin fibreglass board covered on one side with a very thin layer of copper. This is coated with a layer of etch-resistant paint and protected by a thin plastic film.

Unwanted copper is removed leaving a system of copper strips to which the components can be connected.

Making a printed circuit board

1 Trace a copy of the circuit onto acetate sheet to make a mask. Transfer sheets will help you to draw accurate connecting points for the components.

2 Place the mask, face up, on the ultra-violet light box. Peel the backing paper off the laminate and place it on top of the mask. Close the box and expose the laminate for about four minutes.

3 Put on goggles and an apron. Pick up the laminate with tongs and place it carefully into a solution of sodium hydroxide which will remove the exposed etch-resistant paint. Use a brush to gently agitate the solution.

4 When you can see the copper clearly, use tongs to remove the laminate from the solution and wash it thoroughly under running water.

5 Put the laminate into the etching tank basket with the tongs. The tank contains ferric chloride which will dissolve all the uncovered copper.

6 After a few minutes all the unwanted copper will have dissolved. Remove the laminate and wash it thoroughly with runnning water.

7 Use a miniature drill to make holes for the legs of the components. Wear eye protection and make sure that the laminate is held firmly on a piece of wood.

8 Push the legs of the components from the insulated side of the laminate through to the copper strips. Solder them in place.

9 Trim the legs of the components level with the base of the laminate using wire cutters.

Sound is caused by a very fast backward and forward movement called a **vibration**. The vibration sets up a **sound wave** which travels to our ears. All sound waves fade out as they leave the source. However, a sound wave can latch itself onto a **radio wave** and travel huge distances.

We can identify individual sounds because of the different properties which a sound can have.

Components of sound

Volume

Volume is a measure of loudness. The bigger the sound wave the louder the volume.

0 dB	silence
40 dB	quiet class
70 dB	noisy class
95 dB	rock concert

Volume is measured in **decibels (dB)**.

More than 96dB is dangerous and can cause loss of hearing.

Pitch

Sound can be divided into individual notes. The sound wave for each note has a particular **frequency**. This is a measure of the number of peaks or **cycles** that the wave goes through in a given period of time. High pitched notes have a high frequency. Low pitched notes have a low frequency. Humans are able to hear notes ranging from 40 cycles per second up to 20 000 cycles per second. All animals hear a different range of notes.

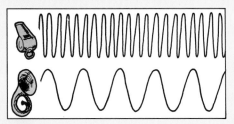

Tone

The shape of the sound wave is altered by the nature of the material or medium through which it travels. The frequency remains the same, but the quality of the note is changed. So although a trumpet and guitar can play the same note their **tones** make them sound quite different.

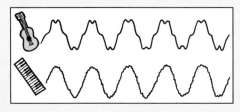

Sound and materials

Sound waves can travel through air, water and other materials.

Hard, shiny, smooth surfaces **reflect** sound. Soft, spongy materials **absorb** sound.

Sound travels especially well along straight-grained wood.

Amplifying sound

You can increase the volume by using one of these **amplifiers**.

Making sound

Any vibration makes a sound. Use any of these methods to set up a vibration.

1 **Blowing into a column of air**. The length of the pipe affects the pitch of the note.

2 **Beating one object with another**. Hollow or springy surfaces produce good sounds.

3 **Plucking or bowing a band or string**. Stretch the string over a sound box. This will usually be  wooden and hollow. Tightening the string raises the pitch of the note. Thicker strings give deeper notes.

4 **Using an electrical impulse**. Switching a circuit on and off very quickly can produce a vibration. Do this using an electromagnet, buzzer or a timer circuit. A computer can be programmed to produce a similar effect.

1 **Funnel** The sound wave bounces between the walls of the funnel.

2 **Sound box** The vibration is transmitted to the sound box by a bridge. A hole in the box lets the amplified sound wave out.

3 All sounds can be passed through an microphone to an **electronic amplifier**.

Light sources

Light rays travel from a **source** and are reflected from different types of surfaces. Every type of material and surface reflects light differently. This is why we see things as different shapes and colors.

1 The **sun** is our main light source.

2 **Hot** objects give off light.

3 **Luminous** materials absorb light which they release in the dark.

4 **Electrical energy** can be converted into light using light bulbs and light emitting diodes (LEDs).

Creating rays

A **narrow beam** of light can be made by blocking out all the light source except for a small hole. A weak light ray needs to be kept in a dark space or it will be lost.

A **wide area** of light can be created by a diffuser. A white translucent plastic sheet or a fine mesh grid will diffuse a light beam.

Color

A **prism** can split white light into its rainbow-colored parts. **Red**, **orange**, **yellow**, **green**, **blue**, **indigo** and **purple**. A **color filter** will only allow its own color of light through. All the other colors will be blocked out.

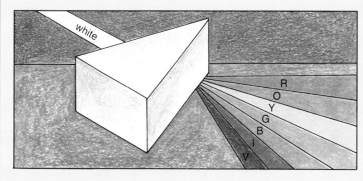

Controlling light rays

Materials

When light falls on an object some of the light is reflected and some is absorbed.

▶ White, smooth and very shiny surfaces **reflect** light.

▶ Black, rough surfaces **absorb** light.

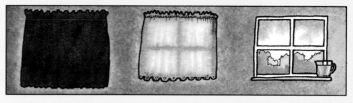

▶ **Opaque** materials do not allow light to pass through so it is impossible to see through them. **Translucent** materials allow light to pass through but it is impossible to see through them. **Transparent** materials allow light to pass through and it is possible to see through them.

▶ Light is bent or **refracted** to different degrees when it passes through different materials.

Mirrors

A mirror reflects all the light which reaches it.

Light rays can be moved around by bouncing them off angled mirrors. A distorted mirror causes strange effects. Two or more mirrors used together create multiple images. Concave and convex mirrors have interesting effects.

Lenses can alter the size of the image.

A system is a set of things which work together. A car is a system and so is a computer.

A way of doing things can also be a system. People working together can form a system.

All systems work the same way.

Something goes into the system. This is called the **input**. Something happens to it. This is called the **process**. Something comes out of the system. This is called the **output**.

Here are some examples:

A production line is a system. Materials come in (**input**) people or robots work (**process**) and products come out (**output**).

Our bodies work by using a combination of systems.

For example, if we have a burn (**input**), nerves send messages to the brain (**process**), and we feel pain (**output**).

Computers are also a combination of systems.

For example, when you press the keys (**input**), the microchips activate (**process**) and the printer prints letters (**output**).

Sometimes the output of a system has an extra effect. The printer may run out of paper, bleep and stop for a refill, the pain might be so great that we faint while the brain readjusts itself, the products may be badly made and have to be returned. This extra output is called **feedback**.

Systems which work well and do not suffer from constant feedback are called **stable** systems. Sensors can be built into a system to keep a check on their performance. These can reduce the effect of feedback. For example, the production line could have quality controllers checking the work at each stage so that products would not need to be returned.

Designers can improve the efficiency of systems by investigating the way that they work. This is called **systems analysis**.

Systems analysis involves separating the system into its individual components. Each bit is looked at carefully to see how it fits in with the rest of the system. Changing one part can have a major effect on the whole system. For example, firing a vandal from the production line would really improve the products!

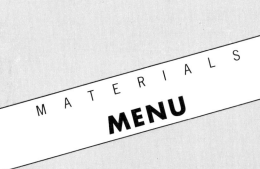

M A T E R I A L S
MENU

In order to make things we need **materials**. Materials have come a long way since the Stone Age. There is a huge range of materials available. Designers have to choose the materials they would like to use. To make a good choice they need to know about the working properties, the costs, the availability, the colors and the visual appeal of materials.

Materials for practical activities can be sorted into four main groups:

Construction

Construction materials need to be tough. They are called resistant materials because they have properties which resist change. They include: wood, metal, plastic, stone, concrete, glass and clay.

Fabric

Fabrics are types of cloth which are made by weaving separate threads or yarns together. Some of the threads which make fabric are wool, cotton, silk, flax, nylon or rayon. Some cloths are made by weaving a combination of these fibers.

Food

The ingredients which make up any type of recipe are called food materials. They can be divided into natural and synthetic food.

Graphic media

The materials for graphics range from paper and cardboard through to video and audio tape, photographic film, paper and chemicals.

Using materials

Materials have to be changed to suit each particular task. This is called **processing** materials.

There are only four ways to process materials.

Addition

For example sewing two bits of canvas together.

Subtraction
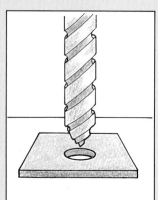

For example, drilling a hole in a piece of wood.

Rearrangement
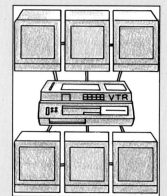

For example, editing a video to alter a sequence.

Forming

For example, pouring liquid jelly into a mould.

Facilities

To process materials we need tools and equipment and the skills that go with them. Learning and developing these skills is a large part of design and technology.

Different materials need different types of facilities. Construction materials tend to create dust and noise. Food materials need hygenic surroundings. Fabric areas need to be clean and light. Graphic media need studio and darkroom facilities. Information technology needs clean, dust-free areas.

Safety

Wherever you are working it is important that you work safely and carefully to avoid accidents and to produce good results. Take note of these points:

1 Don't rush about. Accidents do not save time.

2 Keep your work area tidy. Put things away as soon as you have finished with them.

3 Protect yourself by using the right safety gear.

4 Always carry sharp tools with the point downwards.

5 Make sure that the equipment that you are using is in good condition.

6 You should always be responsible for switching your own machine on or off. Never distract a machinist – wait for them to stop.

7 Always use the right tool for the job. Using the wrong tool causes accidents and spoils work.

Accidents

In case you are the first person on the scene at the accident,

1 Turn off any electrical power.

2 If you have any first aid knowledge, use it.

3 Get help.

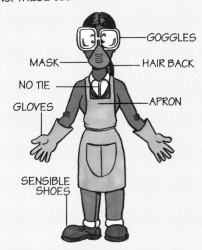

Types of wood

There are two main kinds of wood:

Hardwood

Most hardwood trees have broad leaves which they lose in winter.

Common hardwoods include oak, beech, elm, ash, mahogany, teak and walnut.

General points

▶ Hardwood trees grow more slowly than softwood trees.
▶ Hardwoods are harder and stronger than softwoods.
▶ Hardwoods are more expensive than softwoods.
▶ Hardwoods are more difficult to work than softwoods.

Softwood

Most softwood trees have cones and needles. They are usually evergreen.

Common softwoods include larch, cypress, cedar, spruce, pine and redwood.

Growth

Trees grow by adding an extra layer of wood around the trunk, just under the bark. Two layers are added each year. These account for the **annual rings** which give the age of the tree.

Seasoning

The proportion of water contained in wood is called the **moisture content**. Over a period of time, wood will adjust its moisture content to that of the air around it. If it is drier than the air around it, the wood will swell and warp. If it is wetter then the air around it, the wood will shrink and split. So wood must be dried to suit its intended environment. This drying process is called **seasoning**.

Seasoning can be done in a warm damp oven or outside by natural means.

A plank 1 inch thick takes about two months to dry in an oven and about one year to dry outside.

Environment	Moisture content
Outside	15%–19%
Average interiors	12%–15%
Warm interiors	8%–12%

Conservation

Timber has been a building material for thousands of years. Although it is a renewable material, trees, especially hardwoods, grow very slowly. As a result, the world's forests are declining as demand outstrips supply. Without trees, life on earth could not survive so the remaining forests need to be conserved. As designers it is important for you to recognize this fact and to use wood only where it is appropriate.

Conversion

Logs are sawn up or **converted** into **planks**. Conversion exposes the grain lines in the wood formed by the annual rings.

Wood is also converted into:

▶ Small sections called moldings.

▶ Round sections called dowel.

▶ Thin slices called veneer.

▶ Large boards.

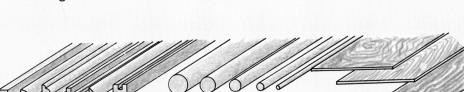

MOLDINGS   DOWEL   VENEER

Man-made boards

Plywood Various qualities depending on the types of wood and glue used in its construction. **Marine ply** is used for underwater jobs. It is very expensive. **Interior ply** is often faced with an attractive veneer on one side. **Multi-ply** is made from many layers. **Particleboard** is cheap plywood made by sandwiching wood fiber between sheets of veneer. Board thicknesses range from ¼ inch to ⅞ inch. Thick sheets of veneer are glued together so that adjoining layers have their grain at 90 degrees to each other.

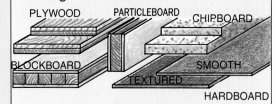

PLYWOOD   PARTICLEBOARD   CHIPBOARD

BLOCKBOARD   SMOOTH

TEXTURED

HARDBOARD

Blockboard These boards are very strong. For interior use only. Board thicknesses are ½, ⅝, ¾, and ⅞ inches. Thin strips of wood are glued together between thick sheets of veneer.

Chipboard For interior use only. Chipboard is cheap but fairly weak and crumbly. Good sharp tools are required to cut it. Board thicknesses are ⅜, ½, ⅝, and ¾ inches. Chippings of wood are mixed with glue and compressed.

Hardboard For interior use only. Hardboard is cheap, thin and flexible. It has rough and smooth faces. Board thicknesses are ⅛, ¼, and ⅜ inches. Wood fiber is glued and compressed into thin sheets.

Data file: Wood

Hardwoods

Oak Hard, heavy timber. Very strong and durable. Expensive. Difficult to work.

Beech Durable, general-purpose, hardwood timber. Kiln-dried beech is often pinkish. Stains well.

Ramin Very plain, straight-grained hardwood. Used extensively for moldings. Stains well.

Mahogany Rich, reddish-brown color. Used for quality furniture.

Softwoods

Redwood Cheap, general-purpose timber, variable quality, not particularly durable.

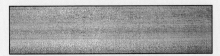

Parana pine Light, plain grain with attractive colored streaks, quite durable. Fairly expensive.

Cedar Sweet smelling, very straight grained. Used to make musical instruments. Expensive.

Metal from rocks

The interior of the earth is liquid rock made from many different elements including metals. When a volcano erupts this liquid pours out onto the surface. As it cools the elements combine and form **rocks**. Rocks which contain a lot of metal elements are called **ores**. Millions of years ago, when the earth was first formed, the same thing happened on a grand scale. Deposits of certain kinds of ore were concentrated in certain areas. These deposits are mined and the ores removed.

Extraction

Metals are removed from their ores by **extraction**. This is usually done by reversing the process of nature. The ores are heated to very high temperatures in a furnace and separated to release the metal. Some ores are also separated using electricity.

Iron was the first metal to be extracted from ores. This is partly because iron ores are very common and partly because the temperature needed to separate the ore is relatively low.

As man learned how to make and control hotter furnaces many more metals became available. Today, as many supplies of ore dwindle and their price goes up, new ways of using metal and substitutes for metal are being developed.

Forms of metals

Liquid metals can be **cast** into molds. Hot metals can be **rolled** into sheets, **drawn** into wires, **extruded** into tubes and bars and **forged** into other shapes.

Properties of metals

General points

► Metals are strong, hard, shiny, heavy and feel cold.
► Metals conduct heat and electricity.
► Some metals are magnetic.
► Metals expand when they are heated.

Improved metals

Alloys

Alloys are made by mixing molten metal with another substance. Alloys are created to form a metallic material with special properties.

Coated metals

One metal can be improved by coating it with another substance.

Alloy	Main elements	Reason
Steel	Iron + carbon	Stronger and harder
Stainless steel	Iron + chromium	Does not rust
Solder	Lead + tin	Lower melting point
Brass	Copper + zinc	Harder, more attractive
Bronze	Copper + tin	Harder, easier to cast

Metal	Coating	Method	Reason
Steel	Chromium	Electrolysis	Resists corrosion/attractive
Steel	Carbon	Case hardening	Hard coating
Aluminium	Aluminium oxide	Electrolysis	Tough coating

Metal: Data file

Metal	Useful properties/ weaknesses	Metal	Useful properties/ weaknesses
Iron	Cheap, brittle, magnetic	Lead	Very soft, heavy, easily shaped, low melting point, resists corrosion, absorbs radiation, highly toxic
Steel	Cheap, strong, rusts, magnetic	Magnesium	Very light, strong, expensive, non-corrosive, used in lightweight alloys
Stainless steel	Expensive, hard, resists rusting, magnetic	Nickel	Magnetic, non-toxic, resists corrosion, strong, used in alloys, expensive
Aluminium	Light, good conductor of heat, soft and easily shaped, non-corrosive, non-toxic	Tin	Expensive, soft, low melting point, resists corrosion, non-toxic, useful in alloys
Copper	Excellent heat and electrical conductor, easily worked, resists corrosion	Titanium	Expensive, very strong and light

Plastic

Plastic is a manufactured material. Unlike wood and metal it does not occur naturally. Plastic is manufactured from crude oil in chemical plants by a process called **fractional distillation**.

Plastic is made up of long molecular chains called **polymers**. They are made almost exclusively of carbon and hydrogen atoms. There are three types of plastic: thermosets, thermoplastics and elastomers. They vary in the way that the polymer chains are held together.

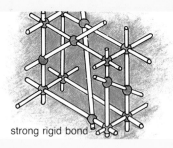
strong rigid bond

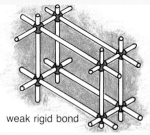
weak rigid bond

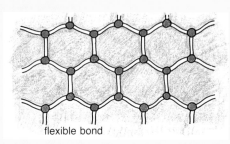
flexible bond

Thermosets

In these plastics the chains are strongly cross-linked. This makes them strong and inflexible. They do not soften with heat and so cannot be reformed. If the heat is too strong it will break the chains and destroy the plastic.

Thermoplastics

These plastics have weakly cross-linked chains. They will soften and bend when heated gently. In this way thermoplastics can be formed into new shapes.

Elastomers

These plastics have such weak bonds between the chains that they are flexible and elastic at normal temperatures.

Industrial processes

Plastic arrives from the chemical works in granule or liquid form. Industrial processes convert the plastic either into more useful forms of plastic material or into finished products. In either case the granules are **plasticised**. This means that they are combined into one solid mass, using heat.

Industrial processes include the following.

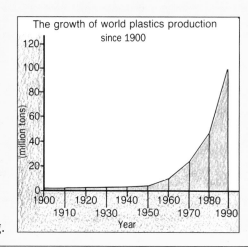
The growth of world plastics production since 1900
(million tons) — Year

History

The first plastic was produced in 1860 but it was not until the 1950's that plastic was used on a commercial scale. Since then, the rise in the use of plastic has been dramatic. Today, plastics are rapidly taking over from the more traditional materials. Plastic technologists are developing new types of plastic with specific properties for specific uses.

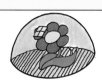

▶ **Extrusion** Granules are warmed, plasticized and pushed out of a nozzle rather like toothpaste out of a tube. Rods, tubes and sheets can be made this way.

▶ **Calendering** Granules are warmed, plasticized and squeezed between rollers. It is rather like rolling out pastry. Flat sheets like polythene sheeting are made in this way.

▶ **Injection molding** Granules are warmed, plasticized, and injected into a closed mold. On cooling the mold opens and a finished article is released. Small items like model kits are made this way.

▶ **Casting** Liquid plastic is mixed with a hardener and poured into a mold. The hardener reacts with the plastic to form a solid cast. The resin is also used to mold fiberglass sheets.

Plastics: data file

Type of plastic	Process method	Examples of use
Thermosets Urea formaldehyde Epoxy resin Polyester resin	Injection molding Casting Casting	Electrical plugs and sockets Glues Boat building
Thermoplastics Acrylic PVC (polyvinylchloride) Nylon Polystyrene Polypropylene	Extrusion/injection molding Compression molding Extrusion/injection molding Foaming, injection molding/calendaring Injection molding/extrusion	Car reflectors LP records Bearings Packaging Milk crates
Elastomers Polyurethane Butyl Silicone	Foaming Extrusion Casting	Foam matresses Cable insulation Electronic components

Plastics in school

Most industrial processes involving plastic cannot be reproduced in the school laboratory. Industrial processes are based on the economics of making many identical items.

However, some forms of plastic can be used and some of the processes can be copied. These include:

Material	Processes
Acrylic sheet	Heat and reform
Polystyrene	Vacuum forming
Nylon	Lathe cutting
Polythene	Heat and reform
Styrofoam	Sculpting
Polyester resin	Casting

Recycling plastics

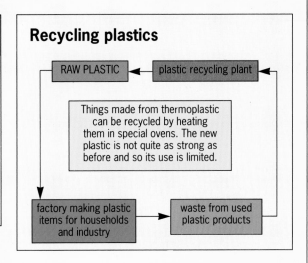

RAW PLASTIC ← plastic recycling plant

Things made from thermoplastic can be recycled by heating them in special ovens. The new plastic is not quite as strong as before and so its use is limited.

factory making plastic items for households and industry → waste from used plastic products

▶ **Foaming** Warm plastic is mixed with compressed air. This expands the plastic by filling it with tiny air pockets. It is a bit like using baking powder to make cakes rise. Foam sponge is made this way.

▶ **Blow molding** A tube of plastic is extruded into a hollow mold. While it is hot, one end of the tube is sealed. Air is blown into the other end so that the plastic tube takes on the shape of the mold. Hollow items like bottles are made this way.

▶ **Vacuum forming** A sheet of plastic is held firmly around the edges and warmed. A vacuum forces the sheet to drape over a prepared mold. It is like sucking in a bubble gum bubble so that it takes on the shape of your face. Masks are made like this.

▶ **Compression molding** Granules are warmed and plasticized. A measured amount is compressed between two halves of a mold. It is like making a toasted sandwich or waffle. Special moldings and blacks are made this way.

Ceramics

Clay is a form of soft rock. When wet it can be shaped and then fired (baked hard) in a kiln. The properties of clay can be altered by adding different substances to it or by coating it with a thin layer of glaze.

Clay is a very ancient material. However, new techniques for molding, firing and glazing clay have made it a very modern material with remarkable properties:

Properties	Uses
Resistance to heat	Space shuttle
Hardness and durability	Engine parts
Insulation	Electronic components

Glass

Glass is molten sand. Hot glass has a texture like molasses. It can be floated to make sheets, blown to make hollow forms and pulled to make thin fibers. Glass fibers can be matted to form a tough, moldable material. New technology uses glass fibers to carry light messages. Glass can be used to cover copper or steel in a process called **enamelling**. Powdered glass or glass strands are melted onto the metal in an enamelling kiln.

Cork

Cork is the bark of the **cork oak** tree. It is very light and is covered in attractive patterns.

Carbon fibre

Carbon fiber is a modern material. Fibers of carbon can be set in resin to make extremely strong and light structures.

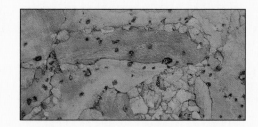

Leather

Leather is the skin of animals. Most leather comes from cow hide. The thick hide is sliced into thin layers. The inner layers are the softest.

Leather is hard-wearing, flexible and can be molded.

Rubber

Rubber is obtained from trees. **Latex** is the raw form of rubber.

Rubber has exceptional grip, stretch and is very flexible. Liquid rubber can be molded.

CONSTRUCTION TECHNIQUES
MENU

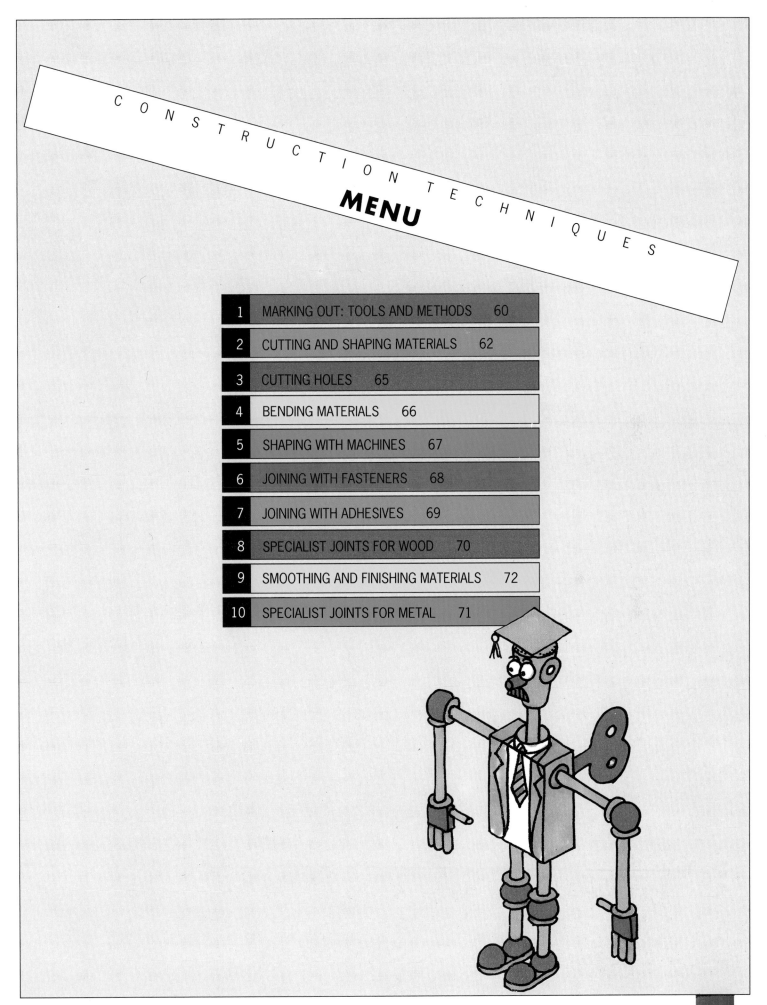

1 MARKING OUT: TOOLS AND METHODS

It is essential to mark out your material carefully before processing it.

Marking out defines:

1 The required shape.
2 Centers of holes.
3 Bends.
4 Joints.

The techniques

Measuring

▶ Use a steel rule. It is made from high quality steel and has an accurate scale. Do not use it as a lever.

▶ Use a steel tape for longer lengths.

▶ Use callipers to measure diameters and thicknesses.

SKILL TIPS

When marking-out:

1 Shade waste material.

2 Keep lines sharp.

3 Make sure the lines are durable.

4 Take care not to damage wanted material.

Markers

Use the right marker for the material.

▲ **Wood** Use a sharp HB pencil. Use a marking knife over the pencil to get a better line.

▲ **Metal** Use a **scriber**. A scriber has a very hard, sharp point. Never hit a scriber with a hammer or the end will snap.

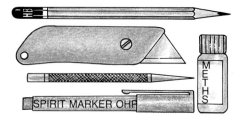

▲ **Plastic** Use a thin, permanent, felt-tipped pen. Make sure you have a suitable solvent in case you need to remove mistakes.

Some plastics can be marked with a pencil.

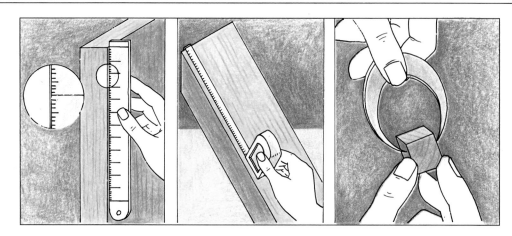

Type of line – tool and method

Straight lines

Use a **steel rule** for short lines. Check to see that the straight edge is true and has no nicks.

Use a steel rule to check if your work is flat. Flat surfaces are marked with this symbol f

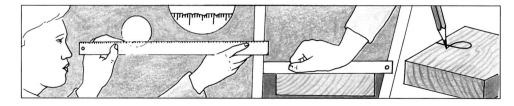

Square lines

Use a **square** for 90 degree lines. Keep the square tight against the edge of the material.

Use a **miter square** for 45 degree lines.

Use a **sliding bevel** for other angles.

Parallel lines

Use a **marking gauge**, with a pencil point or a steel point. Set the distance between the point and the stock. Keep the stock tight against the side of the material. Push the point away to draw a line parallel to the edge. It may help to hold the work in a vice.

On thin sheet material use **odd-leg callipers**. Keep the odd-leg tight against the edge of the material and drag the point along.

Circles

Use a **compass** on wood or **dividers** on metal. Some compasses will hold a thin marker pen. Mark centers with a cross, + and not a dot.

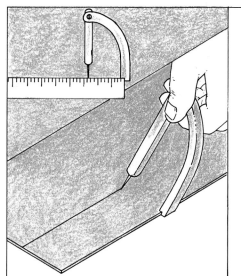

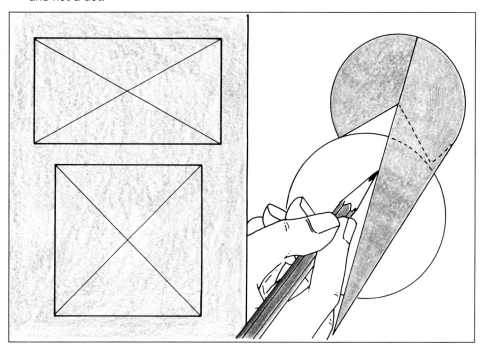

SKILL TIPS

Curves   Bend a thin strip of plywood between two marks. Hold it tightly in position and ask a friend to draw the line.

Finding centers   For rectangular shapes, draw in the diagonals. They will cross at the center.

For circular shapes, use a center finder in two positions

Marking rounded corners

1   Set a marking gauge or odd-leg callipers to the required radius.

2   Mark two lines parallel to the edges. They will cross at the center of the circle.

3   Mark the corner with a compass or dividers.

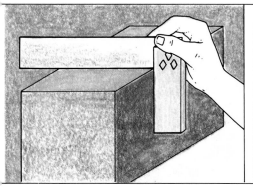

Use a square to check whether two edges are at right angles.

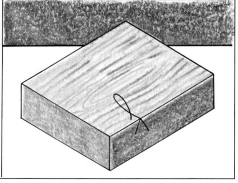

Square edges are marked with this symbol ∨

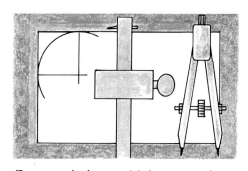

Repeated shapes Make a template from card. Use thin plywood for a more permanent template.

Cutting sheets

The correct cutting tool depends upon the hardness and thickness of the sheet material.

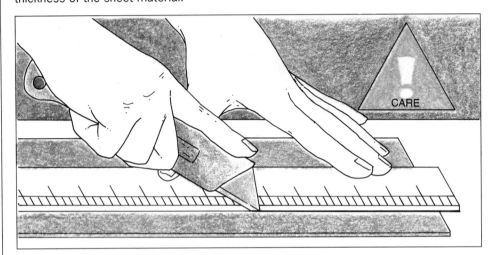

Soft, thin materials

Cardboard, some plastics e.g. corrifoam, corrifulte and veneers.

Use a craft knife and a steel edge. It is best to use a safety rule. Do not try to cut right through the material in one step. Several even strokes are safer and will give you a cleaner cut than one stroke using all your might. A non-slip cutting mat is a useful aid.

SKILL TIP

Tape veneer with scotch tape before cutting it. Cut using very light pressure, especially along the grain.

Thin metal sheet

Use **tinsnips** or a metal cutting **shear**.

SKILL TIP

Hold one handle of the tinsnips in the vice. This will give you one hand to do the cutting and one to hold the sheet.

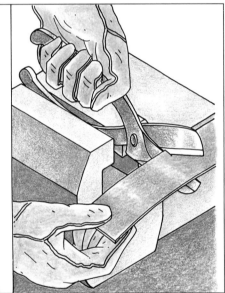

Acrylic sheets

Score and snap

1 Score a groove on the line where you want to cut the sheet. Use a sharp screwdriver or the back of a marking knife against a steel rule. Do not use a craft knife.

2 Hold the sheet in a vise or along or along the edge of a table.

3 Snap firmly! It may pay you to practice on a scrap piece first.

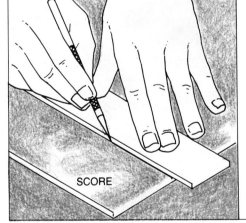

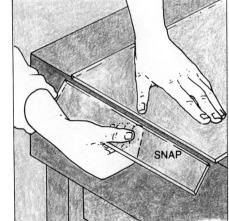

Wood boards

Use the right saw for the job.

General rules

1 The finer the saw teeth the cleaner the cut.

2 The thicker the material the larger the teeth required to cut it.

3 The narrower the blade, the tighter the possible cutting curve.

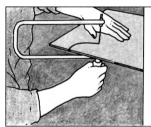  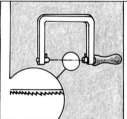  

Types of saw

Fretsaw

This saw has very narrow disposable blades with a choice of tooth sizes. The blades can be changed or inserted into holes to make internal cuts. The large frame and narrow blade can be used to make intricate cuts called **fretwork**.

Coping saw

This saw has a disposable, narrow blade with one general purpose tooth size. Use two hands and hold the work firmly in a vice. The teeth on the blade should point towards the handle so that the saw cuts on a pull stroke. This is a good saw for interior cuts and curves because the blade can be turned or removed and inserted into a hole.

Tenon saw

This saw has a wide blade and is used for straight cuts only. The strengthening rib on the top of the saw makes it impossible for the saw to pass through the sheet. Clamp the sheet firmly on the edge of the bench and saw at a shallow angle.

Panel saw

This saw has a long, wide blade. Use a panel saw for large jobs. A rip saw has particularly large teeth.

Machines for cutting

Electric fretsaw

Remember these points.

1 Use the right saw blade for the job. Check the applications chart.
2 Use goggles and a hold-down arm if it is fitted to the machine.
3 Do not force the material through the saw blade. Let the machine do the work!
4 The blade will get hot and may weld acrylic sheet as it cuts. You may have to cut through twice.

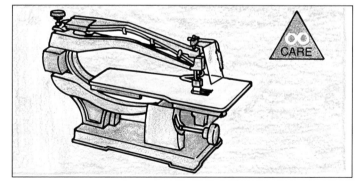

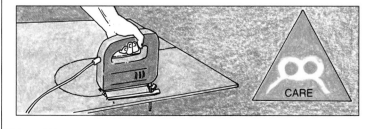

Jig-saw

A jig-saw is portable, allows you to cut large sheets, and is useful for making interior cuts. Points to watch:

1 Make sure you have the right blade for the job.
2 Wear goggles.
3 It is impossible to see underneath the material you are cutting. Make sure you are not cutting the bench or your fingers!

Cutting lengths

For hard materials like metal and plastic use a **hacksaw**. For thinner sections a **junior hacksaw** gives a finer cut. For thicker wood use a **tenon saw** and a sawing board.

For dowel, saw a groove all the way around before cutting through to avoid splitting the wood.

SKILL TIP

When cutting several lengths off one piece.

1 Mark a square end.

2 Measure the required length, square the line and shade the waste material.

3 Cut the length on the waste side of the line.

4 Mark a new square end and repeat as above.

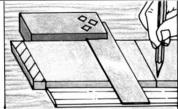
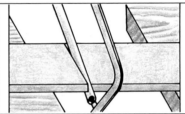

Shaping wood

Planes

Planes have a sharp blade and are used to cut thin slices off wood.

Block plane: for small jobs

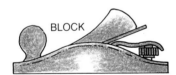

Smoothing plane: for large jobs

Surform: has different shaped disposable blade with many small sharp edges.

Shaping metal and acrylic

Files

A file is used to smooth and shape metal or acrylic. There are a variety of sizes and shapes. Tiny files are called **needle files**.

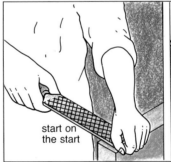
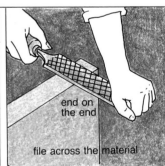

Hold the file at each end and use the whole length of the file while filing the length of the material.

Drills and drill bits

Make sure that the material you are drilling is held down firmly.

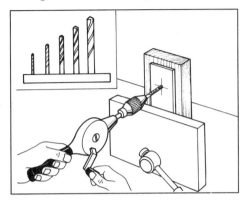

Fix the drill firmly into the chuck. Always mark the center of the hole clearly. Mark the centers on metal with a **center punch**. For big holes, drill a small **pilot hole** first.

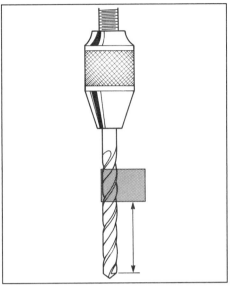

Brace and bit

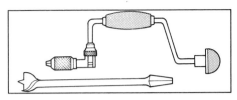

This tool is useful for creating deep wide holes in wood.

Drill in from both sides to get a clean finish.

SKILL TIPS

1 Use tape to help gauge the depth of holes.

2 Support thin materials with a piece of wood.

Drilling machine

A drilling machine can make holes at a particular angle and depth.

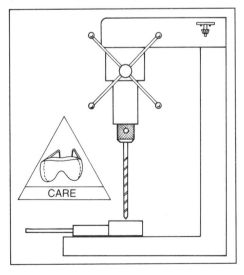

Remember:

1 Always wear goggles.

2 Always hold the work in a vice.

3 Never leave the chuck key in the chuck.

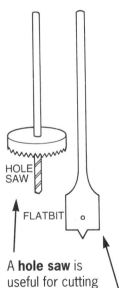

HOLE SAW

FLATBIT

A **hole saw** is useful for cutting large round holes. Ease the saw down gently.

Flatbits are useful for drilling large deep holes into wood.

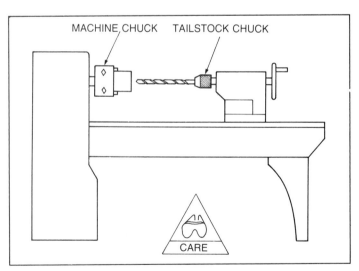

MACHINE CHUCK   TAILSTOCK CHUCK

CARE

Lathe

Drilling holes in the center of round sections can be done accurately on a lathe.

1 Fix the work in the machine chuck.

2 Fix the drill bit into the tailstock chuck.

3 **Wear goggles**.

4 Drive the tailstock drill into the end of the work to the required depth.

4 BENDING MATERIALS

Bending metal – vice and hammer

Hold the metal in a vise and bend the metal using a hammer and a piece of wood. For bends longer than the width of the vise use folding bars. The sheet metal is held by the **folding bars** which are held by the vise. Use a delicate touch to force the metal into a bend. Use a jig or template to get the correct degree of bend.

Thick metal needs to be softened before it will bend. Do this by heating it. Hammer **steel** while it is still hot.

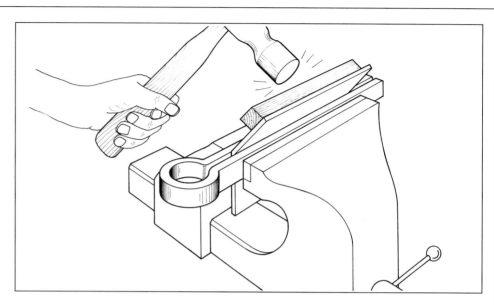

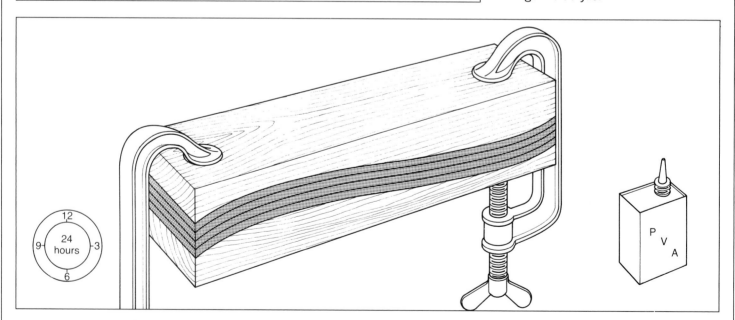

Bending acrylic – strip heater

The strip heater warms a line along the sheet. At a temperature of 169° C the plastic becomes soft and can be bent to the required degree. Use a template or jig to hold the plastic in the correct position until it cools. If the bend is not quite right it can be reheated and changed. **Beware** Overheating will damage the acrylic.

Bending wood – laminating

Thin strips of veneer are glued together and clamped between formers which hold the wood in the required position. The formers are best cut from hardwood. Allow 24 hours for the glue to dry and remove the formers. The glued wood will keep its new shape.

Lathework – general principles

Wood, metal or plastic sections, usually round, are held in the lathe at both ends and revolved. A cutting tool is held against the material, shaping it as it turns.

The speed of the lathe can be increased if the material is perfectly balanced through its center. A faster speed improves the smoothness of the cut.

A lathe is a powerful and dangerous tool. **Always** use eye protection. **Beware** of getting long hair and ties caught in the machinery. Tuck them out of the way.

Wood lathe

The wood is shaped with long-handled, strong chisels. Mark the centers of the ends and fix the wood in between the lathe centers. Hold the chisel firmly with two hands. The front end is supported on the **tool rest** and the handle is used to guide the blade. Different shaped chisels produce different shaped cuts.

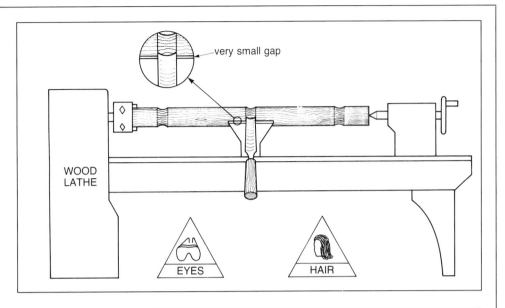

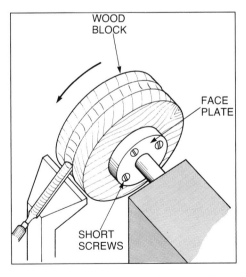

Round wooden blocks can be turned by screwing them to a **face plate**.

The block can be worked from the inside or outside by moving the toolrest. Keep the tool rest as close as possible to the work at all times.

Metal lathe

Metal cutting tools are made from very tough tool steel.

A metal cutting lathe needs to be carefully set up for individual jobs.

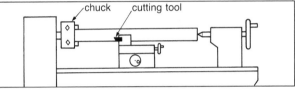

Nylon and acrylic rods can be turned on a metal cutting lathe.

Vacuum former

A vacuum former is a machine used to shape sheet plastic.

1 A sheet of plastic is held firmly around its perimeter above a mold.

2 Heating elements warm the sheet until it is soft and floppy.

3 The air is drawn out from below the sheet causing a vacuum which sucks the soft plastic down and forces it over a prepared mold.

4 When it has cooled, the mold is released together with its plastic copy.

5 The plastic copy is removed from the mold. The excess plastic is trimmed off.

Plastic fixed in place over mold and heated

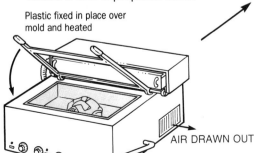

AIR DRAWN OUT

Plastic stretches over mold

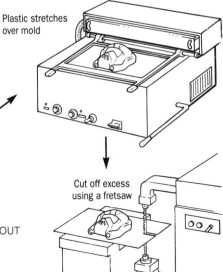

Cut off excess using a fretsaw

6 JOINING WITH FASTENERS

Nails

Nails are used to join things to wood. Nails are often used to keep surfaces tightly pressed together while the glue between them is drying.

Types of nail

Finishing nails Thin nails with small heads which can be easily punched below the wood surface.

Oval heads Oval section nails which avoid splitting the wood. The heads can be punched below the wood surface.

Wire heads General purpose nails with flat round heads which cannot be punched below the wood surface.

Tacks Short tapered nails used to hold fabric and carpet to wood. Their shape makes them easy to remove.

Use a tack hammer for small nails, a heavier hammer for big nails.

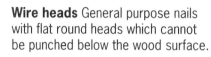

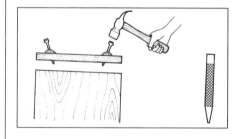

Screws

flathead

slotted head

round head

phil head

self tapper

Screws are used to make temporary holds in wood, or holds which require steady tightening.

Types of screw

Countersunk heads Use a countersink drill to make a funnel shaped hole to fit the screwhead.

Domed heads These extend above the wood.

Self-tapping screws These cut their own thread into metal or plastic.

The screw pulls one surface towards the other. In order to be able to do this, it must be able to turn smoothly. It needs to have a **clearance hole** in the top piece. The hole in the second piece will then guide the screw. It is called a **pilot hole**. It must be big enough to allow the central pillar of the screw to fit. If the pilot hole is too small, the screw will act like a wedge and split the wood.

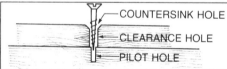

SCREW SIZE	2	4	6	8	10	12
CLEARANCE HOLE	2.0	2.8	3.6	4.2	5.0	5.6
PILOT HOLE	–	1.8	2.0	2.6	2.8	3.0

Sizes in millimeters (mm)

Screw sizes and appropriate holes

Screws are measured by their thickness and length. They can be made from brass, steel or nickel plated steel. They can have slotted heads or phillips heads. It is important to use the correct type and size of screwdriver for the screw.

Nuts, bolts and washers

Make sure the thread on the bolt and the thread on the nut match.

SKILL TIP

If you need to shorten a bolt, screw the nut on first. Saw it with a hacksaw and undo the nut which will clean the thread.

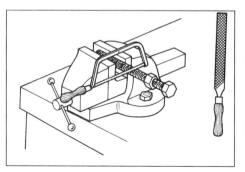

Flat washers spread the load and avoid damage to the materials being joined.

Spring washers and serrated washers stop joints from loosening.

Lock nuts are used to stop a moving part undoing. Use two nuts and tighten one against the other.

SKILL TIPS

1 Use the right glue for the job. General purpose glues tend to produce weaker joins than glues for specific materials. Read the instructions, check the applications, drying times and precautions.

2 A rough surface has a greater gluing area and gives a better grip for the glue to hold.

3 Glues are only effective if the surfaces being glued are in contact with each other. Always apply pressure to the joint until the glue dries using a vice, cramps, weights, sticky tapes, string or nails.

4 Some glues are dangerous. Always protect yourself, your work and your equipment.

Useful glues

White glue (Polyvinylacetate) A non-waterproof glue which forms strong bonds between rigid, porous materials such as wood or cardboard. White paste is used for gluing polystyrene.

Glue gun A fast working glue will fix just about anything. It does not give a very strong hold. It cools and hardens very quickly but it does not form strong bonds so is only useful for small jobs.

Contact cement Bostik, Evostik and Thixofix are examples of this type of glue. It is especially good for large areas. Cover both surfaces with a thin layer. Allow the glue to dry for about 15 minutes and press the surfaces together. You must get the position right first time. **Take care to avoid fumes**, they are unhealthy and inflammable.

Epoxy resin glue Araldite is a good example. These glues are expensive but will glue anything. Mix equal amounts of adhesive and hardener. Spread the glue and clamp the work until the glue hardens. Check the instructions for hardening times.

Rubber solution This glue is specifically used for gluing rubber to rubber. Spread the glue, allow it to dry for about ten minutes, then press the surfaces together.

Tensol cement This glue is specifically for use with acrylic. Take care, use goggles and avoid getting any on your skin. Spread the glue on one surface and clamp the parts together. The glue dissolves the acrylic and then hardens making a weld in the plastic.

Waterproof wood glue Resorcinal resin in an example. This glue is used specifically wood joints which may get wet. Mix the powder with water to make a thick creamy liquid. Apply the glue and clamp overnight.

Latex glue Copydex is an example of a rubber-based glue. Spread the glue on one surface, allow it to dry and press the surfaces together. It is used for fabrics, leather and rubber.

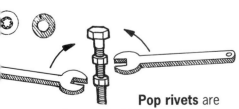

Application chart

	WOOD	METAL	ACRYLIC	POLYSTYRENE	RUBBER	FABRIC
WOOD	PVA CASCAMITE					
METAL	EPOXY RESIN	EPOXY RESIN				
ACRYLIC	EPOXY RESIN	EPOXY RESIN	TENSOL CEMENT			
POLYSTYRENE	PVA paste	PVA paste	PVA paste	PVA paste		
RUBBER	Impact	Impact	Impact	PVA paste	rubber solution	
FABRIC	Copydex	Impact Copydex	Impact Copydex	PVA paste	Copydex	Copydex

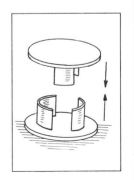

Pop rivets are sometimes called blind rivets because they can be fixed from one side of the material only. Drill the right sized hole for the rivet. Load a rivet into the rivet gun. Squeeze it until the rivet snaps into place.

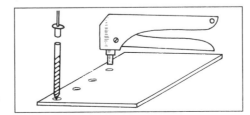

Snap connectors These are useful for lightweight jobs. Two plastic halves are pushed into holes from opposite sides until they lock firmly into place.

8 SPECIALIST JOINTS FOR WOOD

The principles used in these joints can be applied to joining other materials.

Here are four ways to join wood. They all need gluing to make the joints permanent.

Dowelling

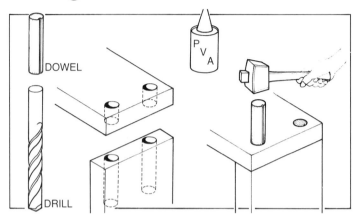

A dowel peg is a round section of wood with a groove down its length.

1 Drill matching holes in the pieces to be joined.

2 Spread glue into the holes and knock the dowel through. Excess glue will be pushed up along the groove in the peg.

3 When the glue is dry, cut the dowels.

4 Smooth the dowels level with the wood using sand paper.

Lap joint

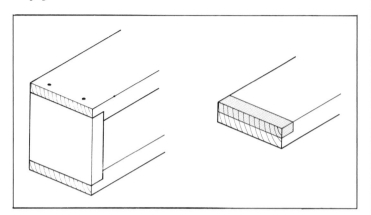

These are useful for corners of box frames. Cutting a step in the end of one piece of wood gives support and a greater gluing area for the other piece.

1 Square a line on the inside of one piece. The distance from the end should equal the thickness of the other piece.

2 Mark a line around the edge at half thickness.

3 Shade the waste and cut out the step.

4 Glue and nail the joint.

Halflap joint

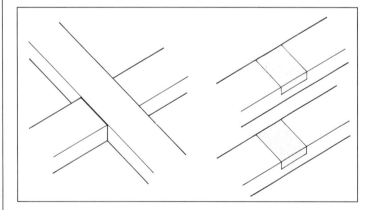

Half the thickness of each piece of wood is removed. This joint useful where two bits of wood cross or meet.

1 Mark out the width and depth of the wood to be removed.

2 Cut across the grain and then either chisel or saw out the step.

3 Glue and nail the two halves.

Dado joint

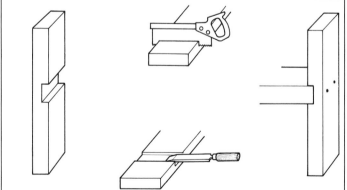

A groove is cut in one piece of wood to house the other piece. The groove width needs to be equal to the thickness of the other piece of wood.

1 Cut the sides of the groove with a tenon saw.

2 Remove the waste wood with a chisel.

3 Glue and nail the joint.

Soft soldering

Heat is used to melt **solder** (an alloy of tin and lead) around two metal parts. When the solder cools and hardens it holds the two parts together. Solder will only stick to the metal if the joint is clean and free from **oxides**. **Flux** is used to stop oxides building up on the metal while it is being heated.

How to solder

1 Clean the surfaces with emery paper.

2 Spread flux around the surfaces to be joined.

3 Heat the joint with a gas torch or hot soldering iron.

4 Apply the solder which will melt around the joint when it is hot enough.

5 Allow the joint to cool.

Soldering electrical components

Electrical components can be soldered with an electric soldering iron. The solder itself usually contains flux.

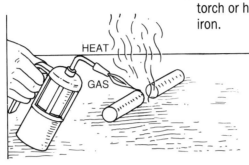

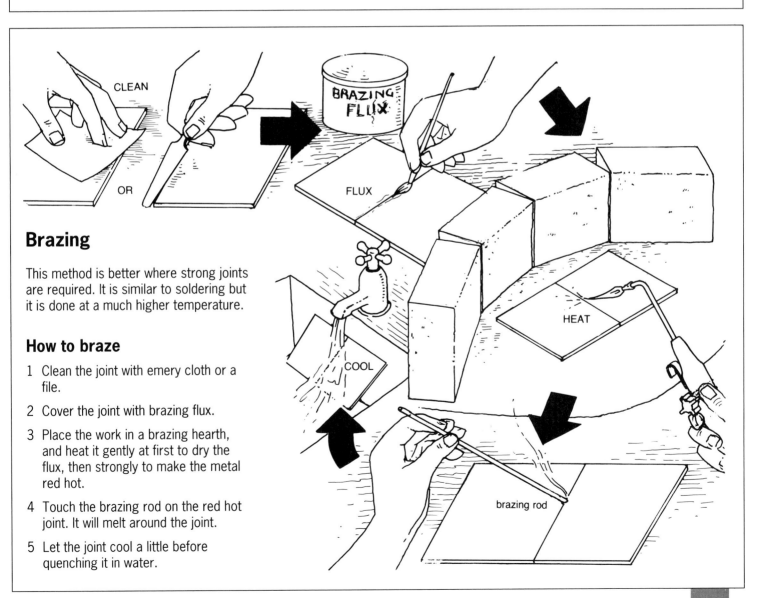

Brazing

This method is better where strong joints are required. It is similar to soldering but it is done at a much higher temperature.

How to braze

1 Clean the joint with emery cloth or a file.

2 Cover the joint with brazing flux.

3 Place the work in a brazing hearth, and heat it gently at first to dry the flux, then strongly to make the metal red hot.

4 Touch the brazing rod on the red hot joint. It will melt around the joint.

5 Let the joint cool a little before quenching it in water.

Smoothing materials

Smoothing a material removes dirt and scratches. It is done in several steps. Do not skip a step. It always takes more time in the long run and the result is never quite as good.

Abrasives

Sandpaper is powdered glass stuck to a sheet of paper. Work through the four grades: coarse (s) → medium (m) → fine (f) → flour.

Wrap a small piece of sandpaper around a cork sanding block and rub along the grain.

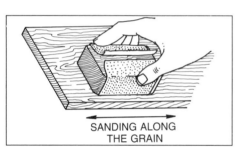

SANDING ALONG THE GRAIN

Wet or dry abrasive paper is silicon carbide grit stuck to waterproof paper. Using it wet avoids dust. Work through the grades: 80 coarse, 240 medium, 600 fine.

Emery cloth Emery cloth is Carburundum powder stuck to cloth. It is tough and flexible. Work through the grades:
coarse → medium → fine.

Avoid using coarse paper on soft metals.

Steelwool   Rub the surface with a pad. Work through the grade:
coarse → medium → fine.

Smoothing machines

Sanding machine

The sanding disc is used for the end-grain of wood. The sanding belt is used along the grain.

Polishing machine

Use eye protection and tuck away long hair and ties. The polisher can only take off the very small scratches left by the abrasive paper. Use an abrasive (**jeweller's rouge**) on the mop and a lubricant (**liquid metal polish**) on the material.

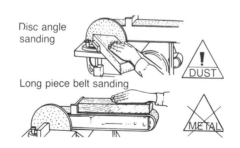

Disc angle sanding

Long piece belt sanding

DUST

METAL

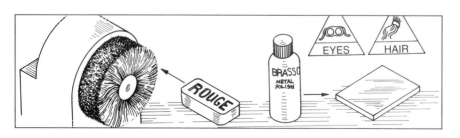

ROUGE

BRASSO METAL POLISH

EYES

HAIR

SKILL TIPS

Smoothing wood

Always work along the grain lines - never across.

1   Plane rough wood.

2   Smooth using sandpaper.

Smoothing metal

Take care with sharp edges.

1   File to smooth rough edges.

2   Use emery cloth to remove file marks.

3   Use steelwool to polish the metal.

Smoothing acrylic

Protect good surfaces to avoid scratching.

1   File to smooth edges.

2   Use wet or dry abrasive paper to remove file marks.

3   Use a polishing machine to finish.

Finishing materials

Paint is like a soup made of tiny colored particles in a liquid called a **solvent**. When paint is spread out thinly, the solvent evaporates leaving the color behind. Different solvents have different drying times.

Most paints need a **primer** coat to help them stick to the material. Use this chart to choose the finish you want.

Paint	Solvent	Approx drying time	Primer	Uses/materials
Poster	Water	30 minutes	None	Wood
Emulsion	Water	4 hours	None	Wood
Gloss	Mineral spirits	12 hours	Yes	Wood/metal
Cellulose	Cellulose thinners	5 minutes	Yes	Wood/metal
Hammerite	Hammerite thinners	10 minutes	No	Metal
Polyurethane varnish	Mineral spirits	4 hours	No	Wood
Acrylic varnish	Water	30 minutes	No	Wood

The trick is to get the paint spread evenly, thinly and, when using fast drying paints, quickly.

Brush

Use a soft brush. Dip in half the brush head and wipe both sides against the side of the can. This will load the brush evenly and stop paint from dripping.

Pull the brush using long even strokes.

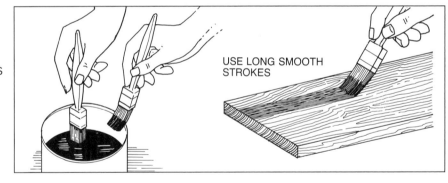

USE LONG SMOOTH STROKES

Spray

Spray cans are expensive but give a better finish than brushes. Mask off areas which you don't want painted.

Varnish

Varnish is a form of transparent, liquid plastic. Apply three coats and rub down with flour paper between coats.

Varnish is available in three types of finish: glossy (very shiny), satin (slightly shiny) and matt (no shine).

Other types of finish

Stains Wood can be stained different shades and colors. The wood grain will show through the color of the stain.

Lacquering Cellulose lacquer is a clear plastic coating. Apply using a spray or brush.

Enamelling Copper can be coated with a decorative layer of glass. Powdered glass is spread on the copper which is baked in an enamelling kiln for 60 seconds at a temperature of 800°C.

Plastic coating Metal can be coated with a thin layer of plastic. The metal is warmed and dipped into plastic powder for a few seconds.

CONTEXT: PERSONAL NEEDS

All people are different and although they have many things in common, they each have their own individual needs.

What sort of personal needs do you have?

The things we do, the way we organize our lives, the way we look and behave make us different from one another.

What other ways make us the individuals that we are?

When we think about ourselves we should not forget about other people. Looking after our own needs does not mean that we have to be selfish.

How do you like people to treat you?

Think about your personal needs and how you might improve your life in some way.

What sort of things are really personal?

LOOKS POSSESSIONS
DATES PROBLEMS ROOM
CLOTHES
FAMILY

SKILLS BOOSTER

The photograph holder

There are many reasons for wanting to display a photograph. It may be to show off a superb picture. it may be a reminder of a special person, place or past event.

Whatever the reason, a photograph always looks better and will last longer if it is properly mounted.

Can you design a holder for your favorite photograph?

Investigation

a What sort of photograph might you want to mount?

b What sort of mounts have you seen or used?

c What sorts of materials might be useful?

Design proposal

1 Choose a photograph or photographs to mount.

2 Suggest some mounting ideas.

3 Select your most promising idea and develop it.

4 Produce a detailed proposal specifying your materials.

Planning and making

▲ Produce a detailed work plan.

▲ Work safely and carefully.

Evaluation

► How does the photograph look? Are you pleased with the result?

► Does it protect the photograph?

► How well did you manage to follow your work plan? Were there any problems?

► How easy is it to change the photograph? Who else do you think might want one?

Bedroom arrangements

The bedroom is one of the places in the house where you can enjoy some privacy. Not everyone is lucky enough to have their own bedroom. There are advantages to sharing a room as long as you can call a part of it your own.

What is your idea of the perfect bedroom?

Healthy living

We all want to be fit and well but we don't always do things which are good for us. In today's world of fast food and fast living, it is easy to develop an unhealthy lifestyle.

How can you keep healthy?

Do you have any other ideas for projects?

Personal adornment

In every country of the world people like to decorate themselves. They have been doing it from the earliest times. Attaching things to their bodies, fixing things to their clothing or painting and decorating their skin. They do it to show status, beliefs, to attract mates, to be fashionable or just to be different.

Investigation

a How do people from other races and cultures adorn themselves?

b What are their reasons?

c How do people in this country adorn themselves? How about you? What are your reasons?

d How do people look after all their bits and pieces of decoration?

Design proposal

1 Sketch out some ideas for personal adornment.

2 Choose an idea that you like and develop it.

3 Produce a detailed design proposal.

Planning and making

▲ Draw up a work plan.

▲ Work carefully and safely.

How do people adorn themselves?

Evaluating

▶ Are you pleased with your work?

▶ How does the finished product compare with the original design?

▶ How closely did you follow your work plan? Did you have any problems?

▶ When will you use your product?

▶ Do you think anyone else would like one?

School is more than a place of learning. It is also where you meet friends and exchange news.

What sort of activities do you do at school?

Education is a system. It is a way of giving pupils knowledge and understanding.

What do you think are the inputs, outputs and controls in the education system?

Many people are involved in the running of a school. Not all of them actually visit the school, many work behind the scenes.

Who are the people involved with school matters? What do they do and where do they work?

Love it or hate it you have to go to school. What sort of school project could you get interested in?

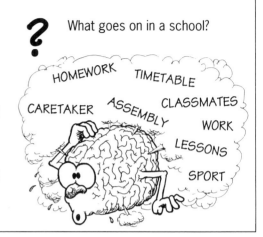

What goes on in a school?

HOMEWORK TIMETABLE CLASSMATES CARETAKER ASSEMBLY WORK LESSONS SPORT

The designer folder

Look after your drawings, keep all your design work and keep everything flat and clean. Feel good about carrying your work between home and school. Give yourself confidence when you are showing your work to other people. These are not easy things to do unless you have a good work folder.

School bags generally have a very short life expectancy. A work folder is particularly vulnerable because of its large, flat shape.

Can you design a folder strong enough to protect your work and smart enough to earn the designer label?

Investigation

a What makes a good folder? What does it need to do? How big does it need to be?

b How will it open and close?

c What sort of materials will work well?

d How can you personalize your folder?

Design proposal

1 Sketch out some ideas.

2 Select your most promising idea and develop it.

3 Draw up a detailed design proposal.

Planning and making

▲ Draw up a work plan.

▲ Work carefully and safely.

Evaluating

▶ Have you given your folder the designer label?

▶ Does it look good, do the papers for this project fit inside?

▶ How closely did you follow your work plan? Did you have any problems?

▶ Do you think your folder will last? Will you use it for you next project?

Pupil facilities

A lot of your time in school is spent out of class. Before school, breakfast, lunch and after school can add up to quite a lot of hours in the week. What do you do with yourself during these times? Could you be getting more out of school?

Which out of lesson facilities do you think are most important?

CLUBS

PLAYGROUND

FREE-TIME FACILITIES

DINNERS

Information

Schools can be very confusing places, especially for new pupils and visitors. People need information so that they can be in the right place at the right time.

What information services should there be in school?

NEWS BULLETIN

TIMETABLE

SCHOOL INFORMATION

SIGNS

Do you have any other ideas for projects?

Protection

Accidents happen all the time. Some accidents are nobody's fault. Some accidents are caused by stupidity or laziness. Some accidents could have been prevented if things were done in a different way. What can be done to make school a safer place?

COTTON WOOL

Investigation

a What is the safety record for your school?

b What are the most common accidents?

c What has been done to reduce them?

d What accidents have you had in your life? Which ones could you have prevented?

Design proposals

1 Decide on the problem area you are going to tackle.

2 Suggest some solutions.

3 Choose one idea and develop it.

4 Produce a detailed design proposal.

Planning and making

▲ Produce a work plan.

▲ Work carefully and safely.

What are the causes of school accidents?

FLOOR SURFACES

SCHOOL CROSSING

SCHOOL ACCIDENTS

SAFETY CAMPAIGN

Evaluating

▶ How do you feel about your product? How does it compare to the original design proposal?

▶ How well did you follow your work plan? Did you have any problems?

▶ Do you think that your idea will prevent accidents? What does your teacher think?

The world has become a smaller place now that travel is so easy and communications are so good. We know a lot more about our planet, how it works and what is happening to it.

How is information about our planet collected and distributed?

People and technology have caused a lot of trouble on earth. Over the centuries many people have made lots of little messes which are now adding up to one big mess.

What sort of world problems have been created by people?
How could these problems have been avoided?

Fortunately, now that we know more about our planet, people are beginning to understand how to look after it.

What sort of project could you do to help preserve our planet?

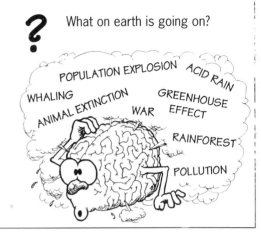
What on earth is going on?

Nuclear flask carrier

Everyone knows how dangerous nuclear accidents can be. Even a small amount of radiation spells disaster. Nuclear power stations run on radioactive fuel and they produce radioactive waste. These have to be carried around the country to be used, reprocessed or stored in relative safety. To do this the radioactive material is carried in special flasks which are designed to be totally leakproof.

Nothing is ever totally safe, but can you design a package to protect something delicate?

Investigation

a What sort of things would you like to protect?

b Why do they need protecting, what might happen to them otherwise?

c How do other people protect delicate things which need to be moved?

Design proposals

1 Choose something which you would like to protect.

2 Decide what you need to protect it from.

3 Choose your most promising idea and develop it.

4 Produce a detailed proposal.

Planning and making

▲ Draw up a work plan.

▲ Work carefully and safely.

Evaluation

► What do you think of your work?

► Does the delicate item fit well? Does it look and feel safe?

► How well did you manage to follow your work plan?

► Did you have to make any changes to it?

► How well do you think your container will work?

► Can you think of a fair test?

► Would you risk it?

Recycling

Why throw useful materials away? When things are finished with, the materials that they are made from can usually be reused. They can be **recycled**.

What, where and how can things be recycled?

Wildlife

Many plants and creatures are dying because their surroundings are being spoiled or destroyed. Whole species are being wiped out as the result of human activity.

What can we do to protect our wildlife?

Do you have any other ideas for projects?

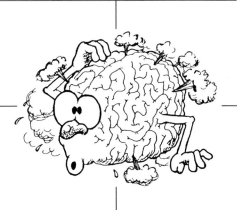

Energy conservation

We use more and more energy in our daily lives. Burning fuel gives off carbon dioxide gas. This gas forms a layer in the upper atmosphere. As this layer gets thicker, it traps more of the Sun's heat. As a result the Earth is getting hotter and more land will turn into desert. Also, as the polar ice caps melt, the seas will get higher and flood low lands.

Investigation

a Where do we use energy?

b Where can energy savings be made?

c Does everyone understand the need for saving energy?

Design proposal

1 Decide on an area of energy conservation which you find interesting.

2 Think about it and suggest some ideas.

3 Select your most promising idea and develop it.

4 Produce a detailed design proposal.

Planning and making

▲ Produce a work plan.

▲ Work safely and carefully.

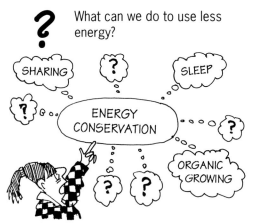

What can we do to use less energy?

Evaluating

► What do you think of the result?

► What do other people think?

► Did you manage to keep to your workplan?

► Will your ideas save energy?

CONTEXT: TRAVEL

Travelling is an essential part of our lives. For all sorts of reasons, people, animals and other things are going places all the time.

Why do people want to travel?
What sorts of things need moving?
Where are they all going?

Travelling and transport systems go together. A bicycle, the railways and a space rocket all depend on systems working well.

What do you think makes a good transport system?

People like to be free to travel, to go where and when they want. However, in fact, our travelling is controlled in many ways.

In what kinds of ways is our freedom to travel controlled?

Travel is a huge project area. What part of it interests you?

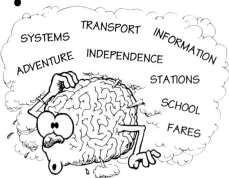

What sort of things does travel bring to your mind?

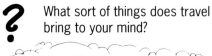

Temporary road signs

Accident!, Road Works!, Gas Leak!. The last thing a driver needs is to come across one of these events without warning. These are some of the situations which require temporary traffic signs to warn drivers and to direct the traffic.

Signs have to be easy to see, simple to understand and be held firmly in place. Temporary signs also need to be easy to store, carry and erect.

Can you design a set of temporary traffic signs to suit a particular road situation?

Investigation

a What sort of road situations require temporary traffic signs?

b How can you use color, size, words and symbols to make signs easy to read and understand?

c How can you ensure that your signs will not be blown down by high winds or passing trucks?

Design proposals

1 Decide upon a road situation and write a clear design brief stating exactly what you are going to design.

2 Draw a sketch map of the road situation and decide upon the signs which you will need to warn and control the traffic.

3 Sketch out some design ideas showing the individual signs.

4 Decide upon the best ideas, choose a suitable scale and produce a detailed design proposal.

Planning and making

▲ Draw up a work plan.

▲ Make scale models of your signs.

▲ Make a suitable display setting for your signs.

Evaluation

► Test your solution.

► Ask drivers to give their opinions. Are the signs easy to see? Will they stay up in high winds?

► How well did they work? Are you pleased with your efforts?

► Who else, apart from road users, could use temporary road signs?

► How could you adapt your signs for other users?

Food for travelers

Everyone needs to eat. Food can give energy when it is needed. A meal can make you sleepy. What, when, how and where should travelers eat?

What should travelers do about eating?

Do you have any other ideas for projects?

Luggage

If you've got something to carry it is called **luggage**. Travelers often have plenty of it! Different things need carrying in different ways so that they don't get lost or damaged.

What should travellers do about the things they carry.

Travel boredom

Traveling can be very boring especially if you cannot move around much. You might be sitting in your seat or waiting at a terminal.

Being bored makes the journey unpleasant and on top of that it makes it seem ten times longer!

Investigation

a Can you remember being bored on a long journey? Why were you bored?

b What are the dangers of travel boredom?

c What sort of things could you do to counter travel boredom?

d How and where would your ideas be used?

Design proposal

1 Decide on a travel situation which you find interesting.

2 Think about and suggest some design ideas.

3 Select your most promising idea and develop it?

4 Produce a detailed design proposal.

What can you do about travel boredom?

Planning and making
▲ Produce a work plan.
▲ Work safely and carefully.

Evaluating
▶ What do you think of the results?
▶ What do other people think?
▶ How did your work plan go?
▶ Try out your idea and see how well it works.

CONTEXT: RECREATION

We all need to relax. It is good to have fun and enjoy yourself after a hard day's work. It refreshes the mind and recharges the body.

Why is it important to relax?

People relax in different ways. One person's idea of enjoyment might be another person's idea of torture.

In what kinds of ways do you relax?

Some types of recreation can be anti-social. What kinds of recreation can be a nuisance to other people?

Money can help, but it is not essential to have it to enjoy yourself. Many forms of recreation are free.

What could you do to have a good time without needing much money?

What sort of recreation project would you enjoy doing?

What does recreation mean to you?

THEATER HOBBIES FUN CLUBS PARKS MUSIC CINEMA GAMES

Bubble blowing machine

Down at the local nightclub the manager is getting worried. Friday and Saturday nights just aren't as busy as they used to be. The music is good but the atmosphere is a little dull.

He decides to spend a lot of money improving the lights and creating special effects to bring back the crowds.

One of the features is to be a bubble-blowing machine. He wants to fill the whole dancefloor with streams of soap bubbles which will catch the light in a million rainbow patterns.

Can you design a machine which will do this?

Investigation

a How is a bubble formed? What affects the size and strength of a bubble? What affects the distance it can travel?

b What would the machine have to look like in order to fit in with other items in the club?

c What sorts of safety features would a bubble making machine in a disco need to have?

Design proposal

1 Experiment to find different ways of making bubbles.

2 Work out ways of making a continuous stream of bubbles.

3 Choose your best idea and develop it.

4 Produce a detailed design proposal.

Planning and making

▲ Make a work plan.

▲ Make a prototype machine with full instructions and possible details of an upgraded machine.

Evaluation

▶ Test your machine. Does it supply a stream of bubbles?

▶ How well does it work?

▶ How easy is it to operate?

▶ How reliable is it?

▶ What is its bubble-blowing capacity?

▶ Where else might your machine be used?

Quiz

TV game shows are always popular. Contestants like them because they are a fun way of testing skills and knowledge. TV companies like them because they are relatively cheap and easy to produce. Audiences like them because they are good entertainment.

? What would you need to produce a good game show?

Going to the beach

Not everyone is lucky enough to have a local beach, but most people get to the beach at some time. The United States has miles of beaches which are used for a wide range of activities.

? What do you need to make the most of the beach?

Do you have any other ideas for projects?

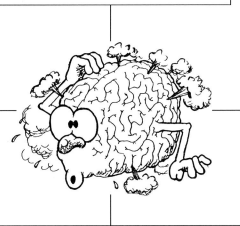

Hobbies

Everyone should have a hobby. It is a constructive way of passing the time in a subject which you find interesting. It's a way of meeting people with similar interests. A hobby is something which you can start and stop as and when the mood takes you.

Investigation

a Choose your hobby and brainstorm the needs.

b Decide on the area which you are going to deal with.

Design proposals

1 Work out some ideas.

2 Choose the best idea and develop it.

3 Produce a detailed design proposal.

Planning and making

▲ Produce a work plan

▲ Work safely and carefully.

Evaluating

▶ Are you pleased with your efforts?

? What do you need for your hobby?

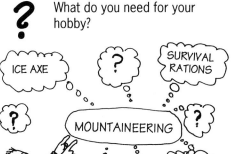

▶ What do other people think of your results?

▶ How well did you manage to keep to your work plan? Were there any problems?

▶ Will you be using your product for your hobby? Could other people use it?

CONTEXT: CELEBRATIONS

People love to celebrate. A success, a chance meting or a traditional event, any excuse will do.

Why do you think people like to celebrate?
Which events do you celebrate?

There are many different ways to celebrate depending on the event. Different countries celebrate events in different ways.

How many ways can you think of for celebrating different events?

Some celebrations are small local affairs. Others are national or even international events.

What do you think is involved in organizing a large international festival?

Can you think of a good project to do with celebrations?

Which occasions do people celebrate?

MOTHER'S DAY
CHRISTMAS BIRTHDAY PRESENTS
CARDS WEDDINGS
NOVELTIES

Pop-up cards

People give cards for all sorts of occasions. A hand-made card has that extra something which cannot be bought. A hand-made card which moves is even more special.

Design and make a pop-up card for a special occasion.

Investigation

a What sort of occasions could you celebrate with a pop-up card?

b How can a pop-up card move?

c What does a card need to say?

Design proposals

1 Choose an event for your card.

2 Decide who it is for.

3 Sketch out some simple ideas.

4 Experiment with pieces of card to develop your best idea.

5 Produce a detailed design proposal.

Planning and making

▲ Draw up a work plan.

▲ Make your card.

▲ Work carefully and safely.

Evaluating

► Are you pleased with your results?

► Does the mechanism work well?

► Could you make any improvements?

► How well did you follow your work plan? Were there any problems?

► Will you mail your card? Do you think it will be appreciated?

Business enterprise

People love to spend money when they are celebrating, even if they cannot afford it. Millions of shoppers cannot help themselves. They flood the stores at Christmas every year. Could you make a business out of a celebration?

How can you make money out of a celebration?

Do you have any other ideas for projects?

Traditions

Often the meaning of a celebration is lost because of all the hype which surrounds it. Events are celebrated in special ways which have been handed down from generation to generation. Can you strengthen or rediscover some old traditions?

What is it that makes a tradition?

Party time

You cannot beat a good party for having fun, relaxing and meeting friends. A party is a great way to celebrate an occasion by bringing people together. If you are going to a party it is worth making an effort preparing.

If you are holding the party it will be up to you to make sure that it is a successful event.

Investigation

a What sort of parties have you been to? What were they like? Were they successful?

b What sort of events are celebrated with parties?

c How can you make one party different from another?

Design proposal

1 Decide on a need for a party. You can decide to do this as a group.

2 Decide on everything you are going to need to make it a successful event. Think of the details as well as the main items.

3 Choose your best ideas and decide on a good way of presenting them.

Planning and making

▲ Draw up a work plan. The timing of events may be very important.

▲ If you are working in a group decide who will be doing what.

What makes a good party?

▲ Work safely and carefully.

Evaluating

► How did you manage with your work plan? Did you have to alter it along the way?

► Was the party a success? What did the partygoers think?

► Did you enjoy the party? Would you hold another one the same?

► Did you have some other ideas which you would have liked to try out?

Home Sweet Home? We all want somewhere which we can call 'home.' It is one of the most basic of all human needs. Home means different things to different people.

What do you need from a home?

The houses which are built today are quite different from those built in the past. Both the places where they can be built and the way they are constructed are strictly controlled.

Why do we need strict building regulations?

The people who live in a home and the things that they do are just as important as the building itself. This is especially important when many people share the same home.

How could you make sure that everyone sharing a home was equally happy?

Can you decide on a project to do with home which would interest you?

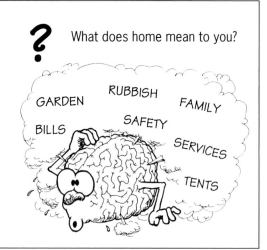

What does home mean to you?

GARDEN · RUBBISH · FAMILY · BILLS · SAFETY · SERVICES · TENTS

Home security

Burglary and theft are on the increase. As people collect more and more things, the more likely they are to be robbed. To counter this, security systems are becoming more advanced. Microchip technology can protect things, detect robbers and alert owners.

Can you develop a security system?

Investigation

a What sort of things need protecting?

b What sort of devices are available? How do they work?

c What do the different systems do?

Design proposal

1 Decide on what you are going to protect and on the system you might use.

2 Work out some ideas.

3 Choose your most promising idea and develop it.

4 Produce a detailed design proposal.

Planning and making

▲ Produce a work plan.

▲ Work safely and carefully.

Evaluating

▶ What do you think of your system?

▶ Does it work?

▶ How closely did you follow your work plan? Did you have any problems?

▶ Do you think the system could be adapted to work out of school? Who else might be interested in your ideas?

Names and addresses

Every person has a name and every home has an address. We want some people to know these details. Sometimes we would rather certain people didn't know them. Do we have any choice?

How do people know our names and addresses?

LETTERS

LABELS

NAMES AND ADDRESSES

PHONE NUMBERS

Pets

Pets can be great fun but they do need looking after. Most pet owners give their animals plenty of love and care.

Unfortunately not all pet owners are responsible enough. Pets have all sorts of needs.

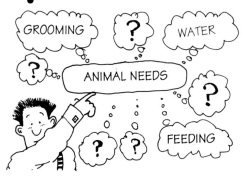

What sort of needs do pets have?

GROOMING

WATER

ANIMAL NEEDS

FEEDING

Do you have any other ideas for projects?

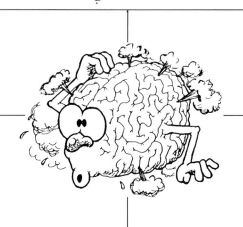

Disaster victims

War, earthquakes, floods and famine. These are just some of the reasons why people are suddenly left without a home. It is hard to imagine the horror of being a disaster victim, yet there are millions of them in the world today.

Investigation

a What kind of disasters have happened recently?

b Who helped and what did they do?

c What problems are there in getting help to the people who need it the most.

Design proposal

1 Choose a need which you would like to help to meet.

2 Sketch out some ideas. Choose your best idea and develop it.

3 Produce a detailed design proposal.

Planning and making

▲ Produce a work plan.

▲ Work safely and carefully.

What help do disaster victims need?

SHELTER

SAFETY

SECURITY

DISASTER VICTIMS

COMFORT

Evaluating

► Are you pleased with your idea?

► What do other people think?

► Did you have any problems with your work plan?

► Do you think your idea could help disaster victims in the future?

► Who might be interested in a good idea?

Businesses exist to make money. We use them to buy the things we need and to get things done. In return we pay money to the owner of the business.

What kinds of business services have you used recently?

Some businesses are much more successful than others. They may make more money, employ more people or simply last longer.

What do you think makes a successful business?

Often a business has two types of people working on it. The people who run the show (the managers) and the people who do the work (the workers).

How could you compare the needs of the managers with the needs of the workers?

Not all business people are simply interested in making money. They have other concerns as well.

What kind of friendly business could you be interested in?

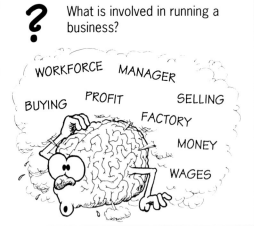

What is involved in running a business?

Product packaging

Walk along any supermarket aisle and you will see containers in all sorts of colors, shapes and sizes. They all shout at you, 'Buy Me!'. Usually people don't spend too much time examining each can, bottle, box or package. They simply pick up the most appealing one. The package advertises the product inside.

When a company has a new product it spends a lot of time and money designing the package.

Can you design the package for a new product? You can choose the product and the name.

Investigation

a What does the package tell you about the product inside?

b How are shape, color, pictures and text used in the packaging?

c What kinds of materials are used in packaging?

Design proposal

1 Choose a product which you would like to package.

2 Look at how different manufacturers have packaged similar products.

3 Sketch out some ideas. Choose your best idea and develop it.

4 Produce a detailed design proposal.

Planning and making

▲ Produce a work plan.

▲ Work carefully and safely.

Evaluating

► What do you think of your packaging?

► Does it look and feel right?

► How well did you follow your work plan? Did you have any problems?

► How does your packaging compare with similar products? Could you try it out on a supermarket shelf?

Production run

In a production line each person does a part of the job. After they have done their part they pass it on to the next person who does the next part of the job. This carries on until the product is completed. It is a team effort. Could you run a production line at school?

What could you produce on a production line at school?

Service industry

A service industry makes money by doing things for people. It can be run by a team or by individuals. It must be clear to people what kind of service is being offered and its important to have the right equipment and facilities for the job.

What kind of service industry could you run from school?

Do you have any other ideas for projects?

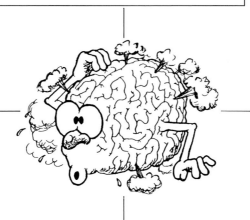

School fundraising

Schools have never had too much cash. Equipment, books and facilities are often in short supply and schools have to raise the cash themselves to buy these essential items. Charities are fundraising all the time. It is a serious business.

Investigation

a In what kind of ways can you raise money?

b How do professional fundraisers collect money?

c What is the money needed for? Where does school fund money go?

d Who could help with your fundraising?

e Are there any laws about fundraising?

Design proposal

1 Work out some fundraising ideas. You might like to work in a team.

2 Choose your best idea and develop it.

3 Produce a detailed design proposal.

Planning and making

▲ Produce a work plan.

▲ Work safely and carefully.

How could you raise money for your school fund?

Evaluating

▶ Are you ready to make money for school?

▶ Did you have trouble with your work plan?

▶ If you worked in a group did you get on well? Were there any difficulties?

▶ How much money do you think you might make for school?

▶ Are you going to give your idea the ultimate test?

Gardens come in all shapes and sizes. In fact they don't even have to be outside. Each kind of garden needs to have different things in it.

How many different kinds of gardens can you think of? What things do these gardens need and where would you get them?

Gardens are definitely good for us and should be encouraged. Gardens give us an opportunity to work with nature to make things grow. They also provide an environment for other things to happen.

What sorts of things can you do in a garden?
What sort of environment would you need in order to do them?

What sort of gardening project might you be interested in?

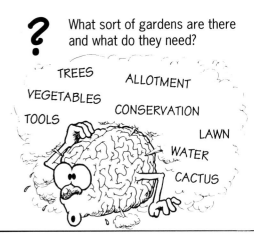

? What sort of gardens are there and what do they need?

TREES
VEGETABLES
TOOLS
ALLOTMENT
CONSERVATION
LAWN
WATER
CACTUS

SKILLS BOOSTER

Garden ornaments powered by natural energy

Garden gnomes may look pretty but they are not very convincing or exciting. Make them move or make a sound and it's a different story. The same applies to other garden ornaments.

Movement requires energy, and it seems an obvious idea to use natural energy to make a garden ornament move.

Can you design an original and interesting garden ornament which is powered by natural energy?

Investigation

a What sorts of natural energy could you use?

b How can they be harnessed? How can they be controlled?

c What sort of ornaments go well in a garden?

d What traditional ideas can you think of? Can you bring any old ideas up to date?

Design proposal

1 Work out some ideas for ornaments and ways to power them.

2 Decide on your best idea. You may have to try a few experiments first.

3 Make a working drawing detailing any mechanisms, systems and materials.

Planning and making

▲ Draw up a work plan.

▲ Make your ornament.

▲ Work carefully and safely.

Evaluation

▶ Test your ornament. How does it look? How well does it work?

▶ What do the neighbors think?

▶ Did your work go according to plan?

▶ How reliably does your ornament work?

▶ Is it a pleasing addition to the garden?

Growing food

Growing food is one of the most satisfying things that a gardener can do. Fresh, home-grown food has a special taste all of its own. It doesn't have to be on a grand scale and there is plenty of food for free in nature's own garden.

Do you have any other ideas for projects?

Protection in the garden

Have you seen the news? 'Prize leeks slashed!' Attacks from vandals, pests, diseases, thorns and the weather can make the garden a dangerous place for plants and gardeners alike.

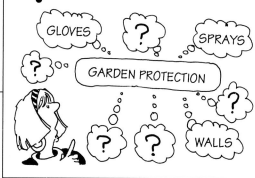

Gardens for handicapped people

Handicapped people often feel cut off. They cannot share the same experiences which many of us take for granted. Yet they need the benefits of nature as much as anyone.

Investigation

a Decide upon the special need which you are going to tackle.

b Where can you find out more information about the problem?

c Put yourself in the place of the handicapped person. What would you like to be able to do?

Design proposal

1 Work out some ideas which would help a handicapped person.

2 Choose your best idea and develop it.

3 Produce a detailed design proposal.

Planning and making

▲ Draw up a work plan.

▲ Work carefully and safely.

Evaluating

▶ How pleased are you with the finished result?

▶ What do other people think?

▶ Did you keep to your work plan? Were there any problems?

▶ Can you try out your idea for someone with special needs?

▶ What do they think? Could more people benefit from your work?

Whether you live in a city or out in the country, you will be part of a local community.

Which area do you think of as your local community?

The people who live in the area make up the local community.

How many people live in your local community?

The local community can offer all kinds of services to help the people who live in it.

What kind of services does you local community provide?
How are these services organized?

Different local communities have different needs.

How do the needs of a seaside town differ from that from a city center?

Can you think of a project which would help your local community?

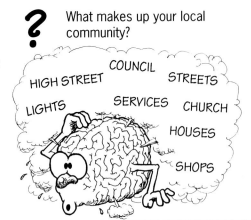

What makes up your local community?

COUNCIL
HIGH STREET   STREETS
LIGHTS   SERVICES   CHURCH
HOUSES
SHOPS

Store fronts

A row of stores in a shopping area can be compared to a row of products on a supermarket shelf. You can tell what a store sells by looking at the way that the store front is designed. You are encouraged to go in and spend your money by the way the store window is dressed.

Town planners try to make sure that the stores in one area look as if they belong together. They also make sure that store fronts suit the buildings in the area.

Choose a particular type of store in a particular type of area and design a store front which will please the storekeeper, the town planner and the public.

Investigation

a Look at your local stores. Choose one type of store to design.

b What sort of image should it have?

c How do stores attract customers?

d How should they match changing fashions?

Design proposals

1 Sketch out some ideas.
2 Choose your most promising idea and develop it.
3 Think about the way you will present your proposals.
4 Produce a detailed proposal.

Planning and making

▲ Draw up a work plan.
▲ Work carefully and safely.

Evaluating

► How pleased are you with your results?
► Do you think you have displayed your proposal well?
► What do other people think?
► How well did you follow your work plan? Did you come across any problems?
► Would your design look good in your local community?
► Would you be proud to suggest it to some local storekeepers?

Community service

We often need our local community services to help us. In the same way we can help other people in our local community. Local councils cannot afford to help as much as they used to. Is there anything we can do to help out?

Do you have any other ideas for projects?

General information

It is all very well having services which can be used by locals and visitors, but do people know what is available? Do they know where things are, who and what to see and how to get there?

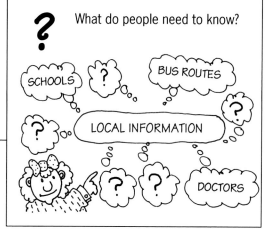

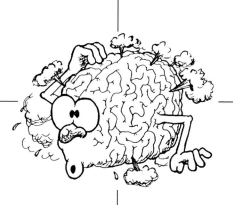

Street facilities

Walk around the local streets and you will see all kinds of objects. These have been put there by storekeepers, local government, engineers and others. These haphazard collections of objects are called street furniture.

Investigation

a Make a list of all the street furniture in your local surroundings.

b Which things are really useful? Which ones are missing?

c How many are in the wrong place? Which ones are well designed?

Design proposal

1 Decide if you are going to design a single item or a whole group of objects.

2 Work out some design ideas.

3 Select your most promising idea and develop it. Choose a suitable scale if you are modelling.

4 Produce a detailed design proposal.

Planning and making

▲ Produce a work plan.

▲ Work carefully and safely.

Evaluation

▶ How pleased are you with your finished selection?

▶ What do other people think?

▶ How well did you follow your work plan? Did you have any problems on the way?

▶ Would your designs improve the local area? How could you get them considered?